The Mountain Bard and Forest Minstrel: Consisting of Legendary Ballads and Songs

James Hogg

MELROSE ABBEY.

THE

MOUNTAIN BARD,

AND

FOREST MINSTREL;

CONSISTING OF

LEGENDARY BALLADS AND SONGS.

BY

JAMES HOGG,

THE ETTRICK SHEPHERD

Fain would I hear our mountains ring
With blasts which former minstrels blew;
Drive slumber hence on viewless wing,
And tales of other times renew.

PHILADELPHIA:

JOHN LOCKEN, 311 MARKET ST.

1851.

1845, 12.
2

1864. may 24

of Bretagne.

(H. C. 1864.)

CONTENTS.

———◆———

THE MOUNTAIN BARD.

THE FOREST MINSTREL.

CLASS FIRST.—PATHETIC SONGS.

iv   CONTENTS.

CONTENTS.

FOREST MINSTREL. CLASS THIRD.—CONTINUED.

CLASS FOURTH.—NATIONAL SONGS.

EXTRACTS.

THE
MOUNTAIN BARD.

SIR DAVID GRÆME.

ANY person who has read the *Minstrelsy of the Scottish Border* with attention, must have observed what a singular degree of interest and feeling the simple ballad of "The Twa Corbies" impresses upon the mind, which is rather increased than diminished by the unfinished state in which the story is left. It appears as if the bard had found his powers of description inadequate to a detail of the circumstances attending the fatal catastrophe, without suffering the interest, already roused, to subside, and had artfully consigned it over to the fancy of every reader to paint it what way he chose; or else that he lamented the untimely fate of a knight, whose base treatment he durst not otherwise make known than in that short parabolical dialogue. That the original is not improved in the following ballad, will too manifestly appear upon perusal; I think it, however, but just to acknowledge, that the idea was suggested to me by reading "The Twa Corbies."

7

SIR DAVID GRÆME.

———

The dow flew east, the dow flew west,
   The dow flew far ayont the fell.
An' sair at e'en she seem'd distrest,
   But what perplext her could not tell.

But aye she cry'd, Cur-dow, cur-dow,
   An' ruffled a' her feathers fair;
An' lookit sad, an' wadna bow
   To taste the sweetest, finest ware.

The lady pined, an' some did blame
   (She didna blame the bonny dow);
But sair she blamed Sir David Græme,
   Wha now to her had broke his vow.

He swore by moon and stars sae bright,
   And by their bed—the grass sae green,
To meet her there on Lammas night,
   Whatever dangers lay between:

To risk his fortune and his life,
   To bear her from her father's ha',
To give her a' the lands o' Dryfe,
   An' wed wi' her for gude an' a'.

9

The day arrived, the evening came,
    The lady look'd wi' wistful ee ;
But, O, alas! her noble Græme
    Frae e'en to morn she could not see.

An' ilka day she sat an grat,
    An' ilka night her fancy wraught,
In wyting this, and blaming that,
    But O the cause she never thought.

The sun had drunk frae Keilder fells
    His beverage o' the morning dew :
The wild-fowl slumber'd in the dells,
    The heather hung its bells o' blue;

The lambs were skipping on the brae,
    In airy notes the shepherd sung,
The small birds hail'd the jocund day,
    Till ilka thicket sweetly rung.

The lady to her window hied,
    That opened owr the banks o' Tyne.
"An' O, alas!" she said, and sigh'd,
    "Sure ilka breast is blithe but mine!

"Where ha'e ye been, my bonny dow,
    That I ha'e fed wi' bread and wine?
As roving a' the country through,
    O saw ye this fause knight o' mine. "

The dow sat on the window tree,
   An' held a lock o' yellow hair;
She perch'd upon that lady's knee,
   An' carefully she placed it there.

"What can this mean? it is the same,
   Or else my senses me beguile!
This lock belong'd to David Græme,
   The flower of a' the British isle.

It is not cut wi' shears nor knife,
   But frae his haffat torn awa:
I ken he lo'ed me as his life,
   But this I canna read at a'.

The dow flew east, the dow flew west,
   The dow flew far ayont the fell,
And back she came, wi' panting breast
   Ere ringing of the castle bell.

She lighted on the hollow tap,
   An' cried Cur-dow, an' hung her wing:
Then flew into that lady's lap,
   An' there she placed a diamond ring.

"What can this mean? it is the same,
   Or else my senses me beguile?
This ring I gave to David Græme,
   The flower of a' the British isle.

" He sends me back the tokens true !
   Was ever maid perplex'd like me ?
'Twould seem h'as rued o' ilka vow,
   But all is wrapt in mystery."

Then down she sat, an' sair she grat ;
   With rapid whirl her fancy wrought,
In wyting this, an' blamin' that ;
   But O the cause she never thought !

When, lo ! Sir David's trusty hound,
   Wi' humpling back, an' hollow ee,
Came cringing in ; an' lookit round,
   Wi' hopeless stare, wha there might be.

He laid his head upon her knee,
   With looks that did her heart assail ;
An' a' that she cou'd flatter, he
   Wad neither bark, nor wag his tail !

She fed him wi' the milk sae sweet,
   An' ilka thing that he wad ha'e,
He lick'd her hands, he lick'd her feet,
   Then slowly, slowly trudged away.

But she has eyed the honest hound,
   An' a' to see where he wad gae :
He stopp'd, and howl'd, an' look'd around,
   Then slowly, slowly, trudged away.

Then she cast aff her coal-black shoon,
　An' sae has she her silken hose;
She kiltit high her 'broider'd gown,
　An' after him in haste she goes.

She follow'd him over muirs and rocks,
　Through mony a dell an' dowy glen,
Till frae her brow, and lovely locks,
　The dew-drops fell like drops o' rain.

An' aye she said, " My love is hid,
　And dare na come the castle nigh;
But him I'll find, an' him I'll chide,
　For leaving his poor maid to sigh;

" But ae press to his manly breast,
　An' ae kiss o' his bonny mou',
Will weel atone for a' the past,
　An' a' the pain I suffer now."

But in a hagg in yonder flow,
　Ah, there she fand her gallant knight!
A loathsome carcass lying low,
　Red-rusted all his armour bright:

Wi' ae wound through his shoulder-bane,
　An' in his bosom twa or three;
Wi' flies an' vermine sair o'ergane,
　An' ugsome to the sight was he.

His piercing een, that love did beet,
   Had now become the raven's prey;
His tongue, that moved to accents sweet,
   Deep frae his throat was torn away.

Poor Reyno fawn'd, an' took his place,
   As glad to see the livid clay;
Then lick'd his master's bloated face,
   An' kindly down beside him lay.

" Now coming was the night sae dark,
   An' gane was a' the light o' day,"
The muir was dun, the heavens mirk,
   An' deep an' dreary was the way.

The croaking raven soar'd on high,
   Thick, thick the cherking weazels ran;
At hand she heard the howlet's cry,
   An' groans as of a dying man.

Wi' horror, an' wi' dread aghast,
   That lady turn'd, and thought o' hame,
An' there she saw, approaching fast,
The likeness o' her noble Græme!

His grim, grim eyelids didna move;
   His thin, thin cheek was deadly pale;
His mouth was black, and sair he strove
   T' impart to her some dreadfu' tale.

For thrice his withered hand he waved,
   An' laid it on his bleedin' breast,
Hast thou a tender heart received?
   How thou wilt tremble at the rest!

Fain wad I tell what there befel,
   But it's unmeet for mortal ear:
The dismal deeds on yonder fell
   Wad shock a human heart to hear.

NOTES TO SIR DAVID GRÆME.

NOTE I.

The dow flew east, the dow flew west.
P. 9, v. 1.

I borrowed the above line from a beautiful old rhyme which I have often heard my mother repeat, but of which she knew no tradition; and from this introduction the part of the dove naturally arose. The rhyme runs thus:

The heron flew east, the heron flew west,
The heron flew to the fair forest;
She flew o'er streams and meadows green,
And a' to see what could be seen:
And when she saw the faithful pair,
Her breast grew sick, her head grew sair;
For there she saw a lovely bower,
Was a' clad o'er wi' lily-flower;

And in the bower there was a bed
With silken sheets, and weel down spread;
And in the bed there lay a knight,
Whose wounds did bleed both day and night;
And by the bed there stood a stane,
And there was set a leal maiden,
With silver needle and silken thread,
Stemming the wounds when they did bleed.

NOTE II.

To gi'e her a' the lands o' Dryfe.

P. 9, v. 5.

The river Dryfe forms the south-east district of
Annandale; on its banks the ruins of the tower of
Græme still remain in considerable uniformity.

NOTE III.

The sun had drunk from Keilder fells
His beverage of the morning dew.

P 10, v. 3.

Keilder Fells are those hills which lie eastward of
the sources of North Tyne.

NOTE IV.

When, lo! Sir David's trusty hound,
With humpling back, and hollow ee.

P. 12, v. 3.

It is not long ago since a shepherd's dog watched
his corpse in the snow amongst the mountains of this
country, until nearly famished, and at last led to the
discovery of the body of his disfigured master.

THE PEDLER.

This Ballad is founded on a fact, which has been magnified by popular credulity and superstition into the
terrible story which follows. It is here related,
according to the *best informed* old people about
Ettrick, as nearly as is consistent with the method
pursued in telling it. I need not inform the reader,
that every part of it is believed by them to be ab-
solute truth.

'Twas late, late, late on a Saturday's night,
   The moon was set, an' the wind was lown;
The lazy mist crept toward the height,
   An' the dim, livid flame glimmer'd laigh on the
      downe.

O'er the rank-scented fen the bittern was warping,
   High on the black muir the foxes did howl,
All on the lone earth the cricket sat harping,
   An' far on the air cam the notes o' the owl.

When the lady o' Thirlestane rose in her sleep,
   An' she shrieked sae loud that her maid ran
      to see;
Her een they war set, an' her voice it was deep,
   And she shook like the leaf o' the aspen tree.

2   17

"O where is the pedler I drave frae the ha',
   That pled sae sair to tarry wi' me?"
"He's gane to the mill, for the miller sells ale,
   An' the pedler's as weel as a man can be."

"I wish he had stay'd, he sae earnestly pray'd,
   And he hight a braw pearling in present to gie;
But I was sae hard, that I would na regard,
   Tho' I saw the saut tear trickle down frae
      his ee.

"But O what a terrible dream I ha'e seen,
   The pedler a' mangled—most shocking to see!
An' he gapit, an' waggit, an' stared wi' his een,
   An' he seemed to lay a' the blame upo' me '

"I fear that alive he will never be seen,
   An' the vera suspicion o't terrifies me:
I wadna hae sickan a vision again
   For a' the guid kye upon Thirlestane lee.

"Yet wha wad presume the poor pedler to kill?
   O, Grizzy, my girl, will ye gang and see?
If the pedler is safe, an' alive at the mill,
   A merk o' guid money I'll gie unto thee."

"O, lady, 'tis dark, and I heard the dead bell!
   And I darna gae yonder for goud nor fee:
But the miller has lodgings might serve yoursel,
   An' the pedler as weel as a pedler can be,"

She sat till day, and she sent wi' fear—
   The miller said there he never had been;
She went to the kirk, and speered for him there,
   But the pedler in life was never mair seen.

Frae aisle to aisle she lookit wi' care;
   Frae pew to pew she hurried her een;
An' a' to see if the pedler was there,
   But the pedler in life was never mair seen.

But late, late, late on a Saturday's night,
   As the laird was walking along the lee,
A silly auld pedler cam bye on his right,
   An' a muckle green pack on his shoulders
      had he.

" O whar are ye gaeing, ye beggarly lown?
   Ye's nauther get lodging nor fall frae me."
He turn'd him about, an' the blude it ran down,
   An' his throat was a' hacker'd, an' ghastly
      was he.

Then straight, wi' a sound, he sank i' the ground,
   A knock was heard, an' the fire did flee;
To try a bit prayer the laird clapped down,
   As flat an' as fear'd as a body cude be.

He fainted: but, soon as he gather'd his breath,
   He tauld what a terrible sight he had seen:
The devil a' woundit, an' bleedin' to death,
   In shape o' a pedler upo' the mill-green.

The lady she shriekit, the door it was steekit,
    The servants war glad that the devil was gane;
But ilk Saturday's night, when faded the light,
    Near the mill-house the poor bleeding pedler
        was seen.

An aye whan passengers bye war gaun
    A doolfu' voice cam frae the mill-ee,
On Saturday's night when the clock struck one,
    Cry'n, " O Rob Riddle, ha'e mercy on me!"

The place was harassed, the mill was laid waste,
    The miller he fled to a far countrie;
But aye at e'en the pedler was seen,
    An' at midnight the voice cam frae the mill-ee.

The lady frae hame wad never mair budge,
    From the time that the sun gaed over the hill;
An' now she had a' the poor bodies to lodge,
    As nane durst gae on for the ghost o' the mill.

But the minister there was a bodie o' skill,
    Nae feared for devil or spirit was he;
An' he's gane awa to watch at the mill,
    To try if this impudent ghaist he cou'd see.

He pray'd, an' he read, an' he sent them to bed;
    Then the Bible anunder his arm took he,
An' round an' round the mill-house he gaed,
    To try if this terrible sight he cou'd see.

Wi' a shivering groan the pedler came on,
  An' the muckle green pack on his shoulders
      had he;
But he nouther had flesh, blude, nor bone,
  For the moon shone through his thin bodye.

The ducks they whackit, the dogs they howl'd,
  The herons they shriekit most piteouslie:
The horses they snorkit for miles around,
  While the priest an' the pedler together might be.

Wi' a positive look he open'd his book,
  An' charged him by a' the sacred Three,
To tell why that horrible figure he took,
  To terrify a' the hale countrie?

" My body was butcher'd within that mill,
  My banes lie under the inner mill-wheel;
An' here my spirit maun wander, until
  Some crimes an' villanies I can reveal:

" I robb'd my niece of three hundred pounds,
  Which providence suffered me ne'er to enjoy;
For the sake of that money I gat my death's
      wounds;
  The miller me kend, but he miss'd his ploy.

' The money lies buried on Balderstone hill,
  Beneath the mid bourack o' three times three.
O gi'e't to the owners, kind sir, an' it will
  Bring wonderful comfort an' rest unto me.

" 'Tis drawing to day, nae mair can I say:
  My message I trust, good father, with thee.
If the black cock should craw, while I am awa,
  O weary, and weary, what wad come o' me!

Wi' a sound like a horn, away he was borne;
  The grass was decay'd where the spirit had
       been:
An' certain it is, from that day to this,
  The ghost of the pedler was never mair seen.

The mill was repaired, and, low in the yird,
  The banes lay under the inner mill-wheel
The box an' the ellwand beside him war hid,
  An' mony a thimble, an' mony a seal.

Must the scene of iniquity cursed remain?
  Can this bear the stamp of the heavenly seal?
Yet, certain it is, from that day to this,
  The millers of Thirlestane ne'er ha'e done
      weel?

But there was an auld mason wha wrought at the
     mill,
  In rules o' providence skilfu' was he;
He keepit a bane o' the pedler's heel,
  An' a queerer wee bane you never did see.

The miller had fled to the forest o' Jed;
  But time had now grizzled his haffets wi' snaw;

He was crookit an' auld, an' his head was turned
    bald,
  Yet his joke he cou'd brik wi' the best o'
    them a'.

Away to the border the mason he ran,
  To try wi' the bane if the miller was fey;
An' into a smiddie, wi' mony a man,
  He fand him a gaffin fu' gaily that day.

The mason he crackit, the mason he taukit,
  Of a' curiosities mighty an' mean;
Then pu'd out the bane, an' declared there were
    nane,
  Who in Britain had ever the marrow o't seen.

When ilka ane took it, an' ilka ane lookit,
  An' ilka ane ca'd it a comical bane;
To the miller it goes, wha, wi' spects on his nose
  To ha'e an' to view it was wonderous fain.

But what was his horror, as leaning he stood,
  An' what the surprise o' the people around,
When the little wee bane fell a streamin wi' blood,
  Which died a' his fingers, an' ran to the ground!

They charged him wi' murder, an' a' the hale
    crew
  Declared, ere they partit, the hale they wad
    ken;

A red goad o' ern fra the fire they drew,
  An' they swore they wad spit him like ony
    muirhen.

"O hald," said the mason, "for how can it be?
  You'll find you are out when the truth I reveal;
At fair 'Thirlestane I gat the wee bane,
  Deep buried anunder the inner mill-wheel.'

"O God," said the wretch, wi' the tear in his ee,
  "O pity a creature lang doom'd to despair;
A silly auld pedler, wha begged of me
  For mercy, I murdered, an' buried him there!"

To Jeddart they haul'd the auld miller wi' speed,
  An' they hangit him dead on a high gallow tree;
An' *afterwards* they in full council agreed,
  That Rob Riddle he richly deserved to dee.

The thief may escape the lash an' the rape,
  The liar and swearer their leather may save,
The wrecker of unity pass with impunity,
  But when gat the murd'rer in peace to the
    gravo?

Ca't not superstition; wi' reason you'll find it,
  Nor laugh at a story attestit sae weel;
For lang ha'e the *facts* in the forest been mindit
  O' the ghaist an' the bane o' the pedler's heel.

NOTES OF THE PEDLER.

NOTE I.

When the lady o' Thirlestane, rose in her sleep.

P. 17, v. 3.

The lady here alluded to was the second wife of Sir Robert Scott, the last knight of Thirlestane.

NOTE II.

O, lady, 'tis dark, and I heard the dead bell!
  An' I darna gae yonder for goud nor fee.

P. 18, v. 6.

By the dead bell is meant a tinkling in the ears, which our peasantry in the country regard as a secret intelligence of some friend's decease. Thus this natural occurrence strikes many with a superstitious awe. This reminds me of a trifling anecdote, which I will here relate as an instance. Our two servant girls agreed to go an errand of their own, one night after supper, to a considerable distance, from which I strove to dissuade them, but could not prevail. So, after going to the apartment where I slept, I took a drinking glass, and, coming close to the back of the door, made two or three sweeps round the lips of the glass with my finger, which caused a loud shrill sound. I then overheard the following dialogue.— B. Ah, mercy! the dead bell went through my head

25

just now, with such a knell as I never heard.—J. I
heard it too!—B Did you, indeed! that is remarkable!
I never knew of two hearing it at the same time
before.—J. We will not go to Midgehope to-night.—
B. I would not go for all the world; I shall warrant it
is my poor brother Wat; who knows what these wild
Irish may have done to him!

Note III.

An' ay' whan passengers bye war gaun,
    A doolfu' voice cam frae the mill-ee,
On Saturday's night, when the clock struck one,
    Cry'n, "O Rob Riddle, ha'e mercy on me!"

P. 20, v. 2.

To account for this, tradition adds, that the miller
confessed, at his death, that the pedler came down to
the mill to inform him that it was wearing late, and
that he must come home to his supper, and that he
took that opportunity to murder him.

Note IV.

The place was harassed, the mill was laid waste.

P. 20, v. 3.

To such a height did the horror of this apparition
arrive in Ettrick, that it is certain there were few in
the parish who durst go to, or by the mill, after sunset.

Note V.

But the minister there was a bodie o' skill,
    Nae feared for devil or spirit was he.

P. 20, v. 5.

The great and worthy Mr. Boston was the person who is said to have laid this ghost; and the people of Ettrick are much disappointed at finding no mention made of it in his memoirs; but some, yet alive, have heard John Corry, who was his servant, tell the following story:—One Saturday afternoon, Mr. Boston came to him, and says, "John, you must rise early on Monday, and get a kilnful of oats dried before day."—"You know very well, master," said John, "that I dare not for my breath go to the mill before day.—"John," said he, "I tell you to go, and I will answer for it, that nothing shall molest you." John, who revered his master, went away, determined to obey; but that very night, said John, he went to the mill, prayed with the family, and stayed very late, but charged them not to mention it. On Monday morning John arose at two o'clock, took a horse, and went to the mill, which is scarcely a mile below the kirk; and, about a bow-shot west of the mill, Mr. Boston came running by him, buttoned in his great coat, but was so wrapt in thought, that he neither perceived his servant nor his horse. When he came home at even, Mr. Boston says to him, "Well, John, have you seen the pedler?"—"No, no, sir," said John, "there was nothing troubled me; but I saw that you were yonder before me this morning." "I did not know that you saw me," said he, "John, nor did I wish to be seen; therefore, say nothing of it." This was in March, and in May following the mill was repaired, when the remains of the pedler and his pack were actually found, and the hearts of the poor people set at ease; for it is a received opinion, that, if the body, or bones, or any part of a murdered person is found, the ghost is then at rest, and that it leaves mankind to find out the rest.

NOTE VI.

He prayed' an' he read, and sent them to bed;
  Then the bible anunder his arm took he,
An' round, an' round the mill-house he gaed,
  To try if this terrible sight he cou'd see.

P. 20, v. 6.

A similar story to this of Mr. Boston and the pedlar
is told of a cotemporary of his, the Reverend Henry
Davieson, of Gallashiels.

NOTE VII.

An' certain it is, from that day to this,
  The millers of Thirlestane ne'er ha'e done weel.

P. 22, v. 2.

Though a pretext can scarcely be found in the an-
nals of superstition sufficient to authorize the ascribing
of this to the murder of the pedlar, so many ages before, yet the misfortunes attending the millers of
Thirlestane are so obvious as to have become prover-
bial: and when any of the neighbours occasionally
mention this, along with it the murder of the pedlar is
always hinted at.

NOTE VIII.

An' *afterwards* they in full council agreed,
  That Rob Riddle he richly deserved to dee.

P. 2 , v. 4.

This alludes to an old and very commom proverb
"that such a one will get Jeddart justice:" which is,
first to hang a man, and then judge whether he was
guilty or not.

GILMANSCLEUCH.

FOUNDED UPON AN ANCIENT FAMILY TRADITION.

"WHAIR ha'e ye laid the goud, Peggye,
   Ye gat on New-Yeir's day?
I lookit ilka day to see
   Ye drest in fine array;

"Bout nouther kirtle, cap, nor gowne,
   To Peggye has come hame;
Whair ha'e ye stowed the goud, dochter?
   I feir ye he have been to blame."

"My goud it was my ain, father;
   A gift is ever free;
And when I neid my goud agene,
   Can it be tint to me?"

"O ha'e ye sent it to a friend?
   Or lent it to a fae?
Or gi'en it to some fause leman,
   To breid ye mickle wae?"

"I ha'e na' sent it to a friend,
   Nor lent it to a fae,
And never man, without your ken,
   Sal cause my joye or wae;

"I ga'e it to a poor auld man,
  Came shivering to the dore;
And when I heard his waesome tale
  I wust my treasure more."

"What was the beggar's tale, Peggye.
  I fain wald hear it o'er;
I fain wald hear that wylie tale
  That drained my little store."

"His hair was like the thistle doune,
  His cheeks were furred wi' tyme
His beard was liké a bush of lyng,
  When silvered o'er wi' ryme;

"He lifted up his languid eye,
  Whilk better days had seen;
And ay he heaved the mournfu' sye,
  While saut teirs fell atween.

"He took me by the hands, and saide,
  While pleasantly he smiled—
O weel to you, my little flower,
  That blooms in desart wilde;

"And may ye never feel the waes
  That lang ha'e followit me;
Bereivit of all my gudes and gear,
  My friends and familye.

" In Gilmanscleuch, beneath the heuch,
   My fathers lang did dwell;
Ay formost, under bauld Buccleuch,
   A foreign fae to quell.

" Ilk petty robber, through the lands,
   They taucht to stand in awe;
And affen checked the plundrin' bands
   Of famous Tushilaw.

" But when the bush was in the flush,
   And fairer there was nane,
Ae blast did all its honours crush,
   And Gilmanscleuch is gane!

" I had ane brither, stout and trew
   But furious, fierce, and keen;
Ane only sister, sweet and young,
   Her name was luvly Jean.

" Hir hair was like the threads of goud,
   Hir cheeks of rosy hew,
Hir eyne war like the huntin' hawk's
   That owr the cassel flew.

" Of fairest fashion was hir form,
   Hir skin the driven snaw,
That's driven by the wintery storm
   On lofty Gilman's-law.

"Hir face a smile perpetual wore,
   Hir teeth were ivorie,
Hir lips the little purple floure
   That blumes on Baillie-lee.

"But, mark! what dool and care, fair maid
   For beauty's but a snare,
Young Jock of Harden her betrayed,
   Whilk greeved us wonder sair.

"My, brother, Adam, stormed and raged,
   And swore in angry mood,
Either to right his dear sister,
   Or shed the traytor's blood.

"I kend his honor fair and firm,
   And didna doubt his faithe,
But, being youngest of seven brethren,
   To marry he was laith.

"When June had deck'd the braes in grene
   And flushed the forest treo:
When young deers ranne on ilka hill,
   And lambs on ilka lee;

"A shepherd frae our mountains hied,
   An ill death mot he dee!
'O master, master, haste,' he cried,
   'O haste alang wi' me!'"

" ' Our ewes are banished frae the glen,
   Their lambs ar drawn away,
The fairest raes on Eldin braes
   Ar Jock of Harden's prey.

" ' His hounds are ringing thro' your wood,
   And manye deer ar slaine ;
A herd is fled to Douglas-Craig,
   Will ne'er returne againe.

" ' Your brother Adam, stout and strong,
   I warned on yon hill-side ;
And he's away to Yarrow's banks.
   As fast as he can ride.'

" O ill betide thy haste, young man !
   Thou micht ha'e tald it me ;
Thou kend, to hunt on all my lande,
   The Harden lads were free.

' Gae, saddel me my milk-white steed,
   Gae, saddel him suddenly ;
To Yarrow banks I'll hie wi' speed,
   This bauld huntir to see.

" But, low, low down, on Sundhop broom,
   My brother Harden spyd ;
And, with a stern and furious look,
   He up to him did ride.

3

" ' Was't not enough, thou traytor strong,
    My sister to betray ?
That thou shouldst scare my feebil ewes,
    And chase the lambs away ?

" ' Thy hounds ar ringing through our woods
    Our choicest deers ar slaine ;
And hundreds fledd to Stuart's hills,
    Wull ne'er returne againe.'

" ' It setts thee weel, thou haughtye youth,
    To bend such taunts on me ;
Oft ha'e you hunted Aikwood hills
    And no man hindered thee.'

" ' But wilt thou wedd my dear sister?
    Now tell me—aye or nay.'
' Nae questions will I answer thee
    That's speerit in sic a way.

" ' Tak this for truth, I ne'er meant ill
    To nouther thee nor thine.'
Then spurrit his steed against the hill,
    Was fleeter than the hynde.

" He set a buglet to his mouth,
    And blew baith loud and cleir ;
A sign to all his merry men
    Their huntin to forbear.

"'O turn thee, turn thee, traytor strong;
 Cried Adam bitterlie;
"'Nae haughtye Scott, of Harden's kin,
 Sal proodlye scool on me.

"'Now draw thy sword, or gi'e thy word,
 For one of them I'll have,
Or to thy face I'll thee disgrace
 And ca' thee coward knave.'

" He sprang frae aff his coal-black steed,
 And tied him to a wande;
Then threw his bonnet aff his head,
 And drew his deidlye brande.

" And lang they foucht, and sair they foucht
 Wi' swords of mettyl kene,
Till clotted blud, in mony a spot,
 Was sprynkelit on the grene.

" And lang they foucht, and sair they foucht,
 For braiver there war nane;
Braive Adam's thye was baithit in blud,
 And Harden's coller bane.

" Though Adam was baith stark and guide,
 Nae longer cou'd he stande;
His hand claive to his hivvye sword,
 His nees plett lyke the wande.

" He leanit himsel ageust ane aek,
   Nae mair cou'd act his parte ;
A wudman then sprang frae the brume,
   And percit young Harden's herte.

" Bein yald and stout, he wheelit about,
   And kluve his head in twaine ;
Then calmlye laid him on the grene,
   Niver to ryse againe.

"I raid owr heicht, I raid through howe,
   And ferr outstrippit the wynde,
And sent my voyce the forest throw,
   But naething cou'd I fynde.

" And whan I came, the dysmal syghte
   Wad melt an herte of stane !
My brither fente and bleiden layé,
   Young Harden neirly gane.

" And art thou there, O Gilmanscleuch !
   Wi' faltren tongue he cried,
Hadst thou arrivit tyme eneuch,
   Thy kinsmen hadna died.

" Be kind unto thy sister Jean,
   Whatever may betide ;
This nycht I meint, at Gilmanscleuch,
   To maik of hir my bride :

" But this sad fraye, this fatal daye,
  May breid baith dule and payne,
My freckle brithren ne'er will staye
  Till they're avengit or slayne.

" The wudman sleeps in Sundhope-brume,
  Into a lowlye grave ;
Young Jock they bure to Harden's tome,
  And layde him wi' the lave.

" Thus fell that brave and cumlye youth,
  Whose arm was like the steel ;
Whose very look was opin truth,
  Whose heart was true and leel.

" It's now full three-and-thirty zeirs
  Syn that unhappye daye,
And late I saw his cumlye corpse
  Without the leist dekaye :

" The garland cross his breast aboon,
  Still held its varied hew ;
The roses bloom'd upon his shoon
  As faire as if they grew.

" I raised our vassals ane and a',
  Wi' mickil care and pain,
Expecting Harden's furious sons
  Wi' all their father's train.

" But Harden was a wierdly man,
    A cunnin' tod was he;
He lockit his sons in prison straung,
    And wi' him bore the key.

" And hee's awa to Holy Rood,
    Amang our nobles a',
With bonnit lyke a girdel braid,
    And hayre like Craighop snaw;

" His coat was like the forest grene,
    Wi' buttons lyke the moon;
His breeks war of the gude buck-skynne,
    Wi' a' the hayre aboon.

" His twa-hand sword hung around his neck,
    And rattled to his heel;
The rowels of his silver spurs,
    Were of the Rippon steel;

" His hose were braced wi' chaine o' hirn,
    And round wi' tassels hung,
At ilka tramp of Harden's heel
    The royal arches rung.

" The courtly nobles of the north
    The chief with wonder eyed,
But Harden's form, and Harden's look,
    Were hard to be denied.

" He made his plaint unto our king,
   And magnified the deed ;
While high Buccleuch, with pith enouch,
   Made Harden better speed.

" Ane grant of all our lands sae fayre,
   The king to him has gi'en,
And all the Scotts of Gilmanscleuch
   War outlawed ilka ane.

" The time I mist, and never wist
   Of nae sic treacherye,
Till I got word frae kind Traquare,
   The country shune to flee.

" For me and mine nae friend wad fynd,
   But fa' ane easy preye ;
While yet my brither weakly was,
   And scarce could brook the way.

" Now I ha'e foucht in foreign fields,
   In mony a bluddy fray,
But lang'd to see my native hills
   Afore my dying day.

" My brother fell in Hungarye,
   When fighting by my side ;
My luckless sister bore ane son
   But broke hir heart and dyed.

" That son, now a' my earthly care,
    Of port and stature fine ;
He has thine eye, and is thy blood,
    As weel as he is mine.

" For me, I'm but a puir auld man,
    That name regairds ava ;
The peaceful grave will end my care,
    Where I maun shortly fa'."——

" I ga'e him a' my goud, father,
    I gat on New Year's day ;
And welcomed him to Harden ha',
    With us awhile to stay."

" My sweet Peggye, my dear Peggye,
    Ye ay were dear to me ;
For ilka bonnet-piece ye gave,
    My love, ye shall ha'e three.

" Auld Gilmanscleuch sal share wi' me
    The table and the ha' ;
We'll tell of a' our doughty deeds
    At hame and far awa.

" That youth, my hapless brother's son,
    Who bears our eye and name,
Sal farm the lands of Gilmanscleuch,
    While Harden halds the same.

" Nae rent, nor kane, nor service mean,
    I'll ask at him at a',
Only to stand at my ryht hand
    When Branxholm gi'es the ca'.

" A Scott should ay support a Scott,
    When sinking to decaye,
'Till over a' the Southlan' hills
    We stretch our ample sway."

THE FRAY OF ELIBANK.

This Ballad is likewise founded on a well known and
well authenticated fact. I am only uncertain what
was. the name of HARDEN's son, who was taken
prisoner, and forced to marry MURRAY's youngest
daughter; but he was either brother or nephew to
him who was slain in Yarrow by the SCOTTS of
Gilmanscleuch.

O WHA hasna heard o' the bauld Juden Murray,
　The lord o' the Elibank castle sae high ?
An' wha hasna heard o' that terrible hurry,
　Whan Wattie o' Harden was catched wi' the
　　kye ?

Auld Harden was ever the king o' gude fellows,
　His tables were filled in the room an' the ha' ;
But peace on the border, that thinned his keyloes,
　And want for his lads, was the warst thing of it a'.

Young Harden was bauld as the Persian lion,
　And langed his skill and his courage to try ;
Stout Willie o' Fauldshope ae night he did cry on,
　Frae danger or peril wha never wad fly.

42

" O Willie ! ye ken our retainers are mony,
  Our kye they rout thin on the loan and the lee ;
A drove we maun ha'e for our pastures sae bonny,
  Or Harden's ae cow aince again we may see.

" Fain wad I, but darena, gang over the border,
  Buccleuch wad restrain us, and ruin us quite ;
He's bound to keep a' the wild marches in order ;
  Then where shall we gae, and we'll venture
    to night ?"

" O master ! ye ken how the Murrays have grund
    you,
  And often caroused on your beef and your veal :
Yet spite o' your wiles and your spies they have
    shunned you—
  A Murray is kittler to catch than the diel !

" Rough Juden o' Eli's grown doited and silly,
  He fights wi' his women frae mornin' till e'en,
Yet three hunder gude kye has the thrifty auld
    billy,
  As fair sleekit keyloes as ever was seen."

" Then, Willie, this night will we herry auld
    Juden ;
  Nae danger I fear while thy weapon I see :
That time when we vanquished the outlaw of
    Sowden,
  The best o' his men were mishackered by thee.

' If we had his kye in the byres of Aekwood,
    He's welcome to claim the best way he can;
But sair he'll be puzzled his title to make good,
    For a' he's a cunning and dexterous man.''

Auld Juden he strayed by the side of a river,
    When the watcher on Hanginshaw-law loud
        did cry—
'' Ho, Juden, take care ! or ye're ruined for ever,
    The bugle of Aekwood has thrice sounded high.''

'' Ha, faith !'' then quo' Juden, '' they're naething
        to lippen,
    I wonder sae long frae a ploy they could cease ;
Gae, blaw the wee horn ; gar my villains come
        trippin' :
    I have o'er mony kye to get rested in peace.''

With that a wee fellow came puffing and blawin',
    Frae high Philip-cairn a' the gate he had run ;—
'' O Juden, be handy, and countna the lawin',
    But warn well, and arm well, or else ye're
        undone !

'' Young Wattie o' Harden has crossed the
        Yarrow,
    Wi' mony a hardy and desperate man ;
The Hoggs and the Brydens have brought him to
        dare you,
    For the Wild Boar of Fauldshop he strides in
        the van.''

"God's mercy!" quo' Juden, "gae blaw the
    great bugle;
  Warn Plora, Traquair, and the fierce Hollowlee.
We'll gi'e them a fleg: but I like that cursed
    Hogg ill,
  Nae devil in hell but I rather wad see.

"To him men in arms are the same thing as
    thistles;
  At Ancram and Sowden his prowess I saw;
But a bullet or arrow will suple his bristles,
  And lay him as laigh as the least o' them a'."

The kye they lay down by the side of the Weel
  On the Elibank craig and the Ashiesteel bourn;
And ere the king's elwand came over the hill,
  Afore Wat and his men rattled mony a horn.

But Juden, as cunning as Harden was strong,
  On ilka man's bonnet has placed a white feather;
And the night being dark, to the peel height they
    thrang,
  And sae closely they darned them amang the
    deep heather.

Where the brae it was steep, and the kye they
    did wend,
  And sair for their pastures forsaken they strave,
Till Willie o' Fauldshop, wi' half o' the men,
  Went aff wi' a few to encourage the lave.

Nae sooner was Willie gane o'er the height,
   Than up start the Murrays, and fiercely set on;
And sic a het fight, in the howe o' the night,
   In the forest of Ettrick has hardly been known.

Soon weapons were clashing, and fire was flashing,
   And red ran the blood down the Ashiesteel bourn;
The parties were shouting, the kye they were
     routing,
   Confusion did gallop, and fury did burn.

But though weapons were clashing, and the fire it
     was flashing,
   Though the wounded and dying did dismally
     groan;
Though parties were shouting, the kye they came
     routing,
   And Willie o' Fauldshop drave heedlessly on!

O Willie, O Willie, how sad the disaster!
   Had some kindly spirit but whispered your ear—
" O Willie, return, and relieve your kind master,
   Wha's fighting, surrounded wi' mony a spear."

Surrounded he was; but his brave little band,
   Determined, unmoved as the mountain they
     stood;
In hopes that their hero was coming to hand,
   Their master they guarded in streams of their
     blood.

In vain was their valour, in vain was their skill,
   In vain has young Harden a multitude slain,
By numbers o'erpowered they were slaughtered at
      will,
   And Wattie o' Harden was prisoner ta'en.

His hands and his feet they ha'e bound like a sheep,
   And away to the Elibank tower they did hie,
And they locked him down in a dungeon sae deep,
   And they bade him prepare on the morrow to die.

Though Andrew o' Langhop had fa'n i' the fight,
   He only lay still till the battle was bye;
Then ventured to rise and climb over the height,
   And there he set up a lamentable cry.—

" Ho, Willie o' Fauldshop! Ho, all is warected!
   Ho! what's to come o' you? or whar are ye gane?
Your friends they are slaughtered, your honour
      suspected,
   And Wattie o' Harden is prisoner ta'en.'

Nae boar in the forest, when hunted and wounded;
   Nae lion or tiger bereaved of their prey,
Did ever sae storm, or was ever sae stounded,
   As Willie, when warned o' that desperate fray.

He threw off his jacket, wi' harness well lined;
   He threw off his bonnet well belted wi' steel;

And off he has run, wi' his troopers behind,
　　To rescue the lad that they likit sae weel.

But when they arrived on the Elibank green,
　　The yett was shut, and the east grew pale;
They slinkit away, wi' the tears i' their een,
　　To tell to auld Harden their sorrowfu' tale.

Though Harden was grieved, he durst venture na
　　　　further,
　　But left his poor son to submit to his fate;
"If I lose him," quo' he, "I can soon get another,
　　But never again wad get sic an estate."

Some say that a stock was begun that night,
　　But I canna tell whether 'tis true or a lie,
That muckle Jock Ballantyne, time of the fight,
　　Made off wi' a dozen of Elibank kye.

Brave Robin o' Singly was killed i' the stoure,
　　And Kirkhope, and Whitsled, and young Bai-
　　　　leylee;
Wi' Juden, baith Gatehop and Plora-fell o'er,
　　And auld Ashiesteel gat a cut on the knee.

And mony a brave fellow, cut off in their bloom,
　　Lie rotting in cairns on the craig and the steele;
Weep o'er them, ye shepherds, how hapless their
　　　　doom!
　　Their natures how faithful, undaunted and leel!

The lady o' Elibank rase wi' the dawn,
 And she wakened auld Juden, and to him did
  say—
"Pray, what will ye do wi' this gallant young
  man?"
 "We'll hang him," quo' Juden, "this very
  same day."

"Wad ye hang sic a brisk and a gallant young heir,
 And has three hamely daughters ay suffering
  neglect?
Though laird o' the best o' the Forest sae fair,
 He'll marry the warst for the sake of his neck.

"Despise not the lad for a perilous feat;
 He's a friend will bestead you, and stand by
  you still;
The laird maun ha'e men, and the men maun ha'e
  meat,
 And the meat maun be had, be the danger what
  will."

Then Juden he leugh, and he rubbit his leg,
 And he thought that the lady was perfectly right.
"By heaven," said he, "he shall marry my Meg;
 I dreamed, and I dreamed o' her a' the last night.'

Now Meg was but thin, an' her nose it was lang;
 And her mou' was as muckle as muckle could be;
Her een they war gray, and her colour was wan,
 But her nature was generous, gentle, and free;

4

Her shape it was slender, her arms they were fine ;
   Her shoulders were clad wi' her lang dusky hair;
And three times mae beauties adorned her mind,
   Then mony a ane that was three times as fair.

Poor Wat, wi' a guard, was brought into a ha',
   Where ae end was black, and the ither was fair ;
There Juden's three daughters sat in a raw,
   And himsel' at the head in a twa-elbow chair :—

" Now, Wat, as ye're young, and I hope ye will
      mend,
   On the following conditions I grant ye your life—
Be shifty, be wearie, be auld Juden's friend,
   And accept of my daughter there, Meg, for your
      wife.

" And since ye're sae keen o' my Elibank kye,
   Ye's hae each o' your drove ye can ken by
      the head ;
And if hae horned acquaintance should kythe to
      your eye,
   Ye shall wale half a score, and a bull for a breed.

" My Meg, I assure you is better than bonny ;
   I reade you in choicing, let prudence decide ;
Then say whilk ye will ; ye are welcome to ony:
   See, there is your coffin, or there is your bride."

"Lead on to the gallows, then," Wattie replied;
  "I'm now in your power, and ye carry it high;
Nae daughter of yours shall e'er lie by my side;
  A Scot, ye maun mind, counts it naething to
    die."

"Amen! then," quo' Juden, "lead on to the tree,
  Your raid ye shall rue wi' the loss of your breath.
My Meg, let me tell ye is better than thee;
  How dare ye, sir, rob us, and lightly us baith?"

When Wat saw the tether drawn over the tree,
  His courage misga'e him, his heart it grew sair;
He watch'd Juden's face, and he watched his ee,
  But the devil a scrap of reluctance was there.

He fand the last gleam of his hope was a fadin';
  The fair face of nature nae mair he wald see.
The coffin was set where he soon must be laid in;
  His proud heart was humbled—he fell on his
    knee!

"O sir, but ye're hurried! I humbly implore ye
  To grant me three days to examine my mind;
To think on my sins, and the prospect before me,
  And balance your offer of freedom sae kind."

"My friendship ye spurned; my daughter ye
    scorned;
  This minute in air ye shall flaff at the spauld:

A preciouser villain my tree ne'er adorned;
 Hang a rogue when he's young, he'll steal nane
  when he's auld.''

'' O sir, but 'tis hard to dash me in eternity
 Wi' as little time to consider my state.''—
'' I swear, then, this hour shall my daughter be
  married t' ye,
 Or else the next minute submit to your fate.''

But Wattie now fand he was fairly warang,
 That marriage to death was a different case.—
'' What matter,'' quo' he, '' though her nose it be
  lang?
 It will ay keep her a bieldly side of a face.

'' To fondle, or kiss her, I'll never be fain,
 Or lie down beside her wi' nought but my sark;
But the first, if I please, I can let it alane;
 And cats they are all alike gray in the dark.

'' What though she has twa little winkling een?
 They're better than nane, and my life it is sweet:
And what though her mou' be the maist I ha'e
  seen?
 Faith, muckle mou'd fook ha'e a luck for their
  meat.''

That day they were wedded, that night they were
    bedded,
  And Juden has feasted them gaily and free;
But aft the bridegroom has he rallied and bladded,
  What faces he made at the big hanging tree.

He swore that his mou' was grown wider than
    Meg's;
  That his face frae the chin was a half a yard
    high;
That it struck wi' a palsy his knees and his legs;
  For a' that a Scott thought it naething to die!

"There's naething," he said, "I more highly
    approve
  Than a rich forest laird to come stealing my kye;
Wad Branxholm and Thirlestane come for a drove,
  I wad furnish them wives in their bosoms to lie."

So Wattie took Meg to the forest sae fair,
  And they lived a most happy and peaceable life:
The langer he kend her, he lo'ed her the mair,
  For a prudent, a virtuous, and sensible wife.

And muckle good blood frae that union has flowed,
  And mony a brave fellow, and mony a brave feat;
I darna just say they are a' muckle mou'd,
  But they rather have a' a good luck for their
    meat.

NOTES TO THE FRAY OF ELIBANK.

—

NOTE.

O wha hasna heard o' the bauld Juden Murray,
The Lord o' the Elibank castle, sae high?

P. 42, v. 1.

Sir Gideon Murray was ancestor of the present Lord
Elibank. The ruins of this huge castle still stand on
the side of a hill, overhanging the Tweed, in the shire
of Selkirk. Lovel Traquair, who was then Murray,
Philliphaugh, Plora, and Sundhope, were all kinsmen
of his; and there is a tradition extant, that all the land
betwixt Tweed and Yarrow once pertained to the potent name of Murray. If so, their possessions must
have bordered a great way with Harden's. The castle
of Aekwood, or Oakwood, the baronial residence of the
latter, stands on the Ettrick, about eight miles south of
Elibank. The other places mentioned are all in that
neighbourhood.

NOTE II.

Stout Willie o' Fauldshop as night he did cry on,
Frae danger or peril wha never wad fly.

P. 42, v. 3.

This man's name was William Hogg, better known
by the epithet of "The Wild Boar of Fauldshop."
Tradition reports him as a man of unequalled strength,

courage and ferocity. He was Harden's chief champion, and in great favour with his master, until once, by his temerity, he led him into a scrape that had well nigh cost him his life. It was never positively said what this scrape was, but there is reason to suppose it was the Fray of Elibank.

NOTE III.

The Hoggs and the Brydens have brought him to dare you. P. 44, v. 5.

The author's progenitors possessed the lands of Fauldshop, under the Scotts of Harden, for ages; until the extravagance of John Scott occasioned the family to part with them. They now form part of the extensive estates of Buccleuch. Several of their wives were supposed to be rank witches.

NOTE IV.

So Wattie took Meg to the forest sae fair. P. 53, v. 4.

Though Elibank is in the shire of Selkirk, as well as Oakwood, yet, originally, by Ettrick Forest, was meant only the banks and environs of the two rivers, Ettrick and Yarrow.

MESS JOHN.

THIS is a very popular story about Ettrick Forest, as well as a part of Annandale and Tweeddale, and is always told with the least variation both by young and old, of any legendary tale I ever heard. It seems, like many others, to be partly founded on facts, with a great deal of romance added; for, if tradition can be in aught believed, the murder of the priest seems well attested: but I do not know if any records mention it. His sirname is said to have been Binram, though some suppose that it was only a nickname; and the mount, under which he was buried, still retains the name of Binram's Corse.

If I may then venture a conjecture at the whole of this story, it is nowise improbable that the lass of Craigyburn was some enthusiast in religious matters, or perhaps a lunatic; and that, being troubled with a sense of guilt, and a squeamish conscience, she had, on that account, made several visits to Saint Mary's Chapel to obtain absolution: and it is well known, that many of the Mountain-men wanted only a hair to make a tether of. Might they not then frame this whole story about the sorcery, on purpose to justify their violent procedure in the eyes of their countrymen, as no bait was more likely to be swallowed at that time? But, however it was, the reader has the story, in the following ballad, much as I have it.

57

MESS JOHN.

Mess John stood in St. Mary's kirk,
   And preached and prayed so mightilie,
No priest nor bishop through the land,
   Could preach or pray so well as he :

The words of peace flowed from his tongue,
   His heart seemed rapt with heavenly flame
And thousands would the chapel throng,
   So distant flew his pious frame.

His face was like the rising moon,
   Imblushed with evening's purple die ;
His stature like the graceful pine
   That grew on Bourhop hills so high.

Mess John lay on his lonely couch,
   And now he sighed and sorely pined ,
A smothered flame consumed his heart,
   And tainted his capacious mind.

It was not for the nation's sin,
   Nor kirk oppressed, that he did mourn ;
'Twas for a little earthly flower—
   The bonny Lass of Craigyburn.

Whene'er his eyes with her's did meet,
   They pierced his heart without remede;
And when he heard her voice so sweet,
   Mess John forgot to say his creed.

"Curse on our stubborn law," he said,
   "That chains us back from social joy;
Those sweet desires, by nature lent,
   I cannot taste without alloy!

"Give misers wealth, and monarchs power;
   Give heroes kingdoms to o'erturn;
Give sophists talents depth to scan—
   Give me the lass of Craigyburn."

Pale grew his cheek, and howe his eye,
   His holy zeal, alas! is flown;
A priest in love is like the grass,
   That fades ere it be fairly grown.

When thinking on her cherry lip,
   Her maiden bosom, fair and gay,
Her limbs, the ivory polished fine,
   His heart, like wax, would melt away!

He tried the sermons to compose,
   He tried it both by night and day;
But all his lair and logic failed,
   His thoughts were aye on bonny May.

He said the creed, he sung the mass,
   And o'er the breviary did turn;
But still his wayward fancy eyed
   The bonny lass of Craigyburn.

One day, upon his lonely couch
   He lay, a prey to passion fell;
And aft he turned—and aft he wished
   What 'tis unmeet for me to tell.

A sudden languor chilled his blood,
   And quick o'er all his senses flew;
But what it was, or what the cause,
   He neither wish'd to know, nor knew:

But first he heard the thunder roll,
   And then a laugh of malice keen;
Fierce whirlwinds shook the mansion-walls,
   And grievous sobs were heard between:

And then a maid, of beauty bright,
   With bosom bare, and claithing thin,
With many a wild fantastic air,
   To his bedside came gliding in.

A silken mantle on her feet
   Fell down in many a fold and turn,
He thought he saw the lovely form
   Of bonny May of Craigyburn'

Though eye and tongue and every limb
   Lay chained as the mountain rock,
Yet fast his fluttering pulses played,
   As thus the enticing demon spoke :—

" Poor heartless man ! and wilt thou lie
   A prey to this devouring flame ?
That thou possess not bonny May,
   None but thyself hast thou to blame.

" You little know the fervid fires
   In female breasts that burn so clear :
The forward youth of fierce desires,
   To them is most supremely dear.

" Who ventures most to gain their charms,
   By them is ever most approved ;
The ardent kiss, and clasping arms,
   By them are ever best beloved.

" Then mould her form of fairest wax,
   With adder's eyes, and feet of horn :
Place this small scroll within its breast,
   Which I, your friend, have hither borne.

" Then make a blaze of alder wood,
   Before your fire make this to stand ;
And the last night of every moon
   The bonny May's at your command.

" With fire and steel to urge her weel,
　　See that you neither stint nor spare;
For if the cock be heard to crow,
　　The charm will vanish into air."

Then bristly, bristly, grew her hair,
　　Her colour changed to black and blue;
And broader, broader, grew her face,
　　Till with a yell away she flew!

The charm was gone: upstarts Mess John,
　　A statue now behold him stand;
Fain, fain, he would suppose 't a dream,
　　But, lo, the scroll is in his hand.

Read through this tale, and, as you pass,
　　You'll cry, alas, the priest's a man!
Read how he used the bonny lass,
　　And count him human if you can.

———

" O Father dear! what ails my heart?
　　Ev'n but this minute I was well;
And now, though ill in health and strength,
　　I suffer half the pains of hell."

" My bonny May, my darling child,
　　Ill wots thy father what to say;

The magic lantern left her head,
  And darkling now return she must.
She wept, and cursed her hapless doom;
  She wept, and called her God unjust.

But on that sad revolving day,
  The racking pains again return!
Ah, we must view a slave to lust,
  The bonny lass of Craigyburn?

Or see her to her father's hall,
  Returning, rueful, ruined quite:
And still, on that returning day,
  Yield to a monster's hellish might?

No—though harassed, and sore distressed
  Both shame and danger she endured:—
For heaven in pity interposed,
  And still her virtue was secured.

But o'er the scene we'll draw a veil,
  Wet with the tender tear of woe;
We'll turn, and view the dire effects
  From this nocturnal rout that flow;

For every month the spectre ran,
  With shrieks would any heart appal;
And every man and mother's son,
  Astonished fled at evening fall.

A bonny widow went at night
   To meet the lad she loved so well;
"Ah, yon's my former husband's sprite!"
   She said, and into faintings fell.

An honest tailor leaving work,
   Met with the lass of Craigyburn;
It was enough—he breathed his last!
   One shriek had done the tailor's turn.

But drunken John of Keppelgill
   Met with her on Carrifran gans;
He, staggering, cried, " Who devil's that ?"
   Then plashing on, cried, " Faith, God kens !"

A mountain preacher quat his horse,
   And prayed aloud with lengthened phiz ;
The damsel yelled—the father smelled—
   Dundee was but a joke to this.

Young Linton, in the Chapelhope,
   Enraged to see the road laid waste,
Way-layed the damsel with a gun,
   But in a panic home was chased.

The Cameronians left their camp,
   And scattered wide o'er many a hill;
Pursued by men, pursued by hell,
   They stoutly held their tenets still.

But at the source of Moffat's stream,
　　Two champions of the cov'nant dwell,
Who long had braved the power of men,
　　And fairly beat the prince of hell:

Armed with a gun, a rowan-tree rung,
　　A bible, and a scarlet twine,
They placed them on the Birkhill path,
　　And distant saw the lantern shine.

And nearer, nearer, still it drew,
　　At length they heard her piercing cries;
And louder, louder, still they prayed,
　　With aching heart, and upcast eyes!

The bible, spread upon the brae,
　　No sooner did the light illume,
Then straight the magic lantern fled,
　　And left the lady in the gloom.

With open book, and haggart look,
　　"Say, what art thou?" they loudly cry;
" I am a woman:—let me pass,
　　Or quickly at your feet I'll die.

"O let me run to Mary's kirk,
　　Where, if I'm forced to sin and shame,
A gracious God will pardon me ;—
　　My heart was never yet to blame."

Armed with the gun, the rowan-tree rung,
   The bible and the scarlet twine,
With her they trudged to Mary's kirk,
   This cruel sorcery out to find.

When nigh Saint Mary's isle they drew,
   Rough winds and rapid rains began,
The livid lightning linked flew,
   And round the rattling thunder ran :

The torrents rush, the mountains quake,
   The sheeted ghosts run to and fro ;
And deep, and long, from out the lake,
   The Water-cow was heard to low.

The mansion then seemed in a blaze,
   And issued forth a sulphurous smell ;
An eldritch laugh went o'er their heads,
   Which ended in a hellish yell.

Bauld Halbert ventured to the cell,
   And, from a little window, viewed
The priest and Satan, close engaged
   In hellish rites, and orgies lewd.

A female form, of melting wax,
   Mess John surveyed with steady eye,
Which ever and anon he pierced,
   And forced the lady loud to cry.

Then Halbert raised his trusty gun,
  Was loaded well with powder and ball,
And, aiming at the monster's head,
  He blew his brains against the wall.

The devil flew with such a clap,
  On door nor window did not stay;
And loud he cried, in jeering tone,
  " Ha, ha, ha, ha, poor John's away!"

East from the kirk and holy ground,
  They bare that lump of sinful clay,
And o'er him raised a mighty mound
  Called Binram's Corse unto this day.

And ay when any lonely wight
  By yon dark cleugh is forced to stray,
He hears that cry at dead of night,
  " Ha, ha, ha, ha, poor John's away."

NOTES TO MESS JOHN.

NOTE I.

Mess John stood in St. Mary's kirk,
> P. 59, v. 1.

The ruins of St. Mary's chapel are still visible, and is in some ancient records, called *The Maiden Kirk*, and, in others, *The Kirk of St. Mary of the Lowes*.

NOTE II.

His stature like the graceful pine,
  That grew on Bourhop-hills so high.
> P. 59, v. 3.

The hills of Bourhop are two thousand feet above the sea's level.

NOTE III.

A silken mantle on her feet
  Fell down in many a fold and turn.
> P. 61, v. 6.

It is a vulgar received opinion, that, let the devil assume what appearance he will, were it even that of an angel of light, yet still his feet must be cloven.

71

NOTE IV.

With fire and steel to urge her weel,
See that you neither stint nor spare.

                                   P. 63, v. 1.

The story says, that the priest was obliged to watch
the picture very constantly; and that always when the
parts next the fire began to soften, he stuck pins into
them, and exposed another side; that, when each of
these pins were stuck in, the lady uttered a piercing
shriek; and that, as their number increased in the
waxen image, her torment increased, and caused her to
hasten on with amazing speed.

NOTE V.

Where wild Polmoody's mountains tower,
Full many a wight their vigils keep.

                                   P. 64, v. 5.

The mountains of Polmoody, besides being the highest, are the most inaccessible in the south of Scotland;
and great numbers from the western counties, found
shelter on them during the heat of the persecution.

NOTE VI.

Where roars the torrent from Loch-skene,
A troop is lodged in trenches deep.

                                   P. 64, v. 5.

There are sundry cataracts in Scotland, called *The
Gray Mare's Tail*; in particular, one in the parish of

Closeburn, in Nithsdale : and one betwixt Stranraer
and Newton-Stewart : but that in Polmoody, on the
border of Annandale surpasses them all ; as the water,
with only one small intermission, falls from a height of
300 yards. This, with the rocks overhanging it on each
side, when the water is flooded, greatly excels any
thing I ever saw in awful grandeur. Immediately
below it, in the straitest part of that narrow pass which
leads from Annandale into Yarrow, a small strong
intrenchment is visible. It is called by the country
people *The Giant's trench.* It is in the form of an oc-
tave, and is defended behind by a bank. As it is not
nearly so much grown up as those at Philiphaugh, it
is probable, that a handful of the covenanters might
fortify themselves there during the time that their
brethren were in arms. But it is even more probable,
that a party of the king's troops might be posted for
some time in that important pass ; as it is certain,
Claverhouse made two sweeping circuits of that
country, and, the last time, took many prisoners in
the immediate vicinity of this scene. May we not
likewise suppose, that the outrage committed at Saint
Mary's kirk might contribute to his appearance in
those parts?

Note VII.

Young Linton in the Chapelhope,
Enraged to see the road laid waste.
P. 67, v. 5.

The Lintons were, in those days, and even till toward the beginning of the last century, the principal

farmers in all the upper parts of Ettrick and Yarrow; yet such a singular reverse of fortune have these opulent families experienced, that there is now rarely one of the name to be found above the rank of the meanest labourer.

NOTE VIII.

But at the source of Moffat's stream,
 Two champions of the cov'nant dwell;
Who long had braved the power of men,
 And fairly beat the prince of hell.

P. 68, v. 1.

These men's names were Halbert Dobson, and David Dun; better known by those of Hab Dob, and Davie Din. The remains of their cottage is still visible, and sure never was human habitation contrived on such a spot. It is on the very brink of a precipice, which is 400 feet perpendicular height, whilst another of half that height overhangs it above. To this they resorted, in times of danger, for a number of years: and the precipice is still called *Dob's linn*.

There is likewise a natural cavern in the bottom of the linn farther up, where they, with other ten, hid themselves for several days, while another kept watch upon the Path-know; and they all assembled at the cottage during the night.

Tradition relates farther of these two champions, that, while they resided at the cottage by themselves, the devil appeared to them every night, and plagued them exceedingly; striving often to terrify them, so as to make them throw themselves over the linn. But

one day they contrived a hank of red yarn in the form
of crosses, which it was impossible the devil could
pass; and, on his appearance at night, they got in
behind him, and attacked him resolutely with each a
bible in one hand, and a rowan-tree staff in the other,
and, after a desperate encounter, they succeeded in
tumbling him headlong over the linn; but, to prevent
hurting himself at the moment he was overcome, he
turned himself into a batch of skins!

Note IX.

And deep and long, from out the lake
The Water-cow was heard to low,

P. 69, v. 3.

In some places of the Highlands of Scotland, the
inhabitants are still in continual terror of an imagi-
nary being, called *The Water-Horse.*

Note X.

And forced the lady loud to cry.

P. 69, v. 6.

The lass of Craigyburn after this line, is no more
mentioned: but the story adds, that she died of a
broken heart, and of the heats which she got in,
being forced to run so fast.

THE

DEATH OF DOUGLAS,

LORD OF LIDDISDALE.

———

THE first stanza of this Song, as well as the history of
the event to which it refers, is preserved by Hume
of Godscroft in his history of the House of Douglas.
The author having been successful in rescuing some
excellent old songs from the very brink of oblivion,
searched incessantly many years after the remains of
this, until lately, by mere accident, he lighted upon a
few scraps, which he firmly believes to have formed
a part of that very ancient ballad. The reader may
judge for himself. The first verse is from Hume;
and all those printed within brackets are as near the
original as rhyme and reason will permit. They are
barely sufficient to distinguish the strain in which the
old song hath proceeded.

———

THE Lady Douglas left her bower,
　　An' ay sae loud as she did call,
" 'Tis all for gude Lord Liddisdale
　　That I do let these tears down fall."

[" O haud your tongue, my sister dear,
　An' o' your weepin' let me be :
Lord Liddisdale will haud his ain
　Wi' ony Lord o' Chrystendie.

" For him ye widna weep nor whine
　If you had seen what I did see,]
That day he broke the troops o' Tyne,
　Wi's gilded sword o' metal free.

" Stout Heezlebrae was wonder wae
　To see his faintin' vassals yield ;
An' in a rage he did engage
　Lord Liddisdale upon the field.

" 'Avaunt, thou haughty Scot,' he cry'd,
　' Nor dare to face a noble fae :
Say—wilt thou brave the deadly brand,
　And heavy hand of Heezlebrae !'

" The word was scarcely mixt wi' air,
　When Douglas' sword his answer gae ;
An' frae a wound, baith deep and sair,
　Out fled the soul o' Heezlebrae.

" Mad Faucet next, wi' wounds transfixt,
　In anguish gnaw'd the bloody clay ;
Then Hallinshed he wheil'd an' fled,
　An' left his rich, ill-gotten prey.

"I ha'e been west, I ha'e been east,
   I ha'e seen dangers many a ane;
But for a bauld and dauntless breast,
   Lord Liddisdale will yield to nane.

"An' were I called to face the foe,
   An' bidden chuse my leader free;
Lord Liddisdale would be the man
   Should lead me on to victory.

[" O haud your tongue, my brother John!
   Though I have heard you patientlie,
Lord Liddisdale is dead an' gone,
   An' he was slain for love o' me.

"My little true an' trusty page
   Has brought the heavy news to me,
That my ain lord did him engage
   Where he could nouther ficht nor flee.

"Four o' the foremost men he slew,
   An' four he wounded despratelie;
But cruel Douglas came behind,
   An' ran him through the fair bodie.]

"O wae be to the Ettrick wood!
   O wae be to the banks of Ale!
O wae be to the dastard croud
   That murder'd handsome Liddisdale!

[" It wasna rage for Ramsey slain
    That raised the deadly feid sae hie ;]
Nor perjur'd Murray's timeless death—
    It was for kindness shown to me.

[" When I was led through Liddisdale,
    An' thirty horsemen guarding me ;
When that gude lord came to my aid,
    Sae soon as he did set me free !]

" The wild bird sang, and woodlands rang,
    An' sweet the sun shone on the vale ;
Then thinkna ye my heart was wae
    To part wi' gentle Liddisdale.

" But I will greet for Liddisdale,
    Until my twa black een rin dry ;
An' I will wail for Liddisdale,
    As lang as I ha'e voice to cry.

" And for that gude lord I will sigh
    Until my heart an' spirit fail ;
An', when I die, O bury me
    On the left side of Liddisdale."

" Now haud your tongue, my sister dear,
    Your grief will cause baith dule an' shame
Since ye were fause, in sic a cause,
    The Douglas' rage I canna blame."

"Gae stem the bitter norlan' gale;
　Gae bid the wild wave cease to rowe;
I'll own my love for Liddisdale
　Afore the king, my lord, an' you."

He drew his sword o' stained steel,
　While neid-fire gleam'd frae ilka eye,
Nor pity, nor remorse did feel,
　Till dead she at his feet did lye.

" O cruel man! what ha'e I done?
　I never wrong'd my lord nor thee;
I little thought my brother John
　Could ha'e the heart to murder me."

Sunk was her een, her voice was gane,
　Her bonny face was pale as clay,
Her hands she rais'd to heaven for grace;
　Then fainted, sank, and died away.

He dight his sword upon the ground;
　Wi' tentless glare his een did rowe,
Till fixing on the throbbing wound
　That stain'd her breast of purest snow.

He cry'd, "O lady, fause an' fair!
　Now thou art dead and I undone!
I'll never taste of comfort mair,
　Nor peace of mind, aneath the sun.

6

" Owr mountains, seas, an' burnin' sand,
    I'll seek the plains of Italie;
Then kneel in Judah's distant land,
    An' syne come back an' sleep wi' thee."

WILLIE WILKIN.

THE real name of this famous warlock was Johnston; how he came to acquire that of Wilkin I can get no information, though his name and his pranks are well known in Annandale and Nithsdale. He seems to have been an abridgment of Mr Michael Scott; but, though his powers were exhibited on a much more narrow scale, they were productive of actions yet more malevolent.

THE glow-worm goggled on the moss
    When Wilkin rode away,
And much his aged mother fear'd,
    But wist not what to say.

For near the change of every moon,
    At deepest midnight tide,
He hied him to yon ancient fane
    That stands by Kinnel side.

His thoughts were absent, wild his looks,
    His speeches fierce and few;
But who he met, or what was done,
    No mortal ever knew.

83

"O stay at home, my only son!
　O stay at home with me!
I fear I'm secretly forewarn'd
　Of ills awaiting thee.

"Last night I heard the dead-bell sound,
　When all were fast asleep;
And ay it rung, and ay it sung,
　Till all my flesh did creep.

"And when on slumber's silken couch
　My senses dormant lay,
I saw a pack of hungry hounds,
　Would make of thee their prey.

"With feeble step I ran to help,
　Or death with thee to share;
When straight you bound my hands and feet
　And left me lying there.

"I saw them tear thy vitals forth;
　Thy life-blood dyed the way;
I saw thy eyes all glaring red
　And closed mine for ay.

"Then stay at home, my only son!
　O stay at home with me!
Or take with thee this little book,
　Thy guardian it shall be."

"Hence, old fanatic, from my sight!
   What means this senseless whine?
I pray thee mind thine own affairs,
   Let me attend to mine."

"Alas, my son! the generous spark
   That warm'd thy tender mind
Is now extinct, and malice keen
   Is only left behind.

"How canst thou rend that aged heart
   That yearns thy woes to share?
Thou still hast been my only grief,
   My only hope and care.

"Ere I had been one month a bride,
   Of joy I took farewell;
With Craigie, on the banks of Sark,
   Thy valiant father fell.

"I nurs'd thee on my tender breast,
   With mickle care and pain;
And saw, with pride, thy heart expand,
   Without one sordid stain.

"With joy, each night, I saw thee kneel
   Before the throne of grace;
And on thy Saviour's blessed day
   Frequent his holy place.

" But all is gone! the vespers sweet
  Which from our castle rose
Are silent now, and sullen pride
  In hand with envy goes!

" Thy wedded wife has sway'd thy hear
  To pride and passion fell;
O! for thy pretty children's sake,
  Renounce that path of hell.

" Then stay at home, my only son!
  O with thy mother stay!
Or tell me what thou goest about,
  That for thee I may pray."

He turn'd about, and hasted out,
  And for his horse did call;
" An hundred fiends my patience rend
  But thou excell'st them all."

She slipt beneath his saddle lap
  A book of psalms and pray'rs,
And hasten'd to yon ancient fane,
  To listen what was there.

And when she came to yon kirk-yard,
  Where graves are green and low,
She saw full thirty coal-black steeds
  All standing in a row.

Her Willie's was the tallest steed,
  'Twixt Dee and Annan whole;
But plac'd beside that mighty rank,
  He kyth'd but like a foal.

She laid her hand upon his side;
  Her heart grew cold as stone!
The cold sweat ran from every hair,
  He trembled every bone!

She laid her hand upon the next,
  His bulky side to stroke,
An' ay she reach'd, and ay she stretch'd—
  Was nothing all but smoke.

It was a mere delusive form
  Of films and sulphry wind;
And every wave she gave her hand
  A gap was left behind.

She pass'd through all those stately steeds,
  Yet nothing marr'd her way,
And left her shape in every shade,
  For all their proud array

But whiles she felt a glowing heat,
  Though mutt'ring holy prayer;
And filmy veils assail'd her face,
  And stifling brimstone air.

Then for her darling desperate grown,
   Straight to the aisle she flew;
But what she saw, and what she heard,
   No mortal ever knew.

But yells, and moans, and heavy groans,
   And blackest blasphemye,
Did fast abound; for every hound
   Of hell seem'd there to be.

And after many a horrid rite,
   And sacrifice profane,
" A book! a book!" they loudly howl'd;
   " Our spells are all in vain.

" Hu! tear him, tear him limb from limb,"
   Resounded through the pile,
" Hu! tear him, tear him straight, for he
   Has mocked us all this while."

The tender matron, desperate grown,
   Then shriek'd most bitterlye:
" O spare my son, and take my life,
   The book was lodged by me."

" Ha! that's my frantic mother's voice!
   My life or peace must end:
O take her! take her!" loud he cried,
   " Take her, and spare thy friend!"

The riot rout then sallied out,
　　Like hounds upon their prey ;
And gathered round her in the aisle
　　With many a hellish bray.

Each angry shade endeavours made
　　Their fangs in blood to stain,
But all their efforts to be felt
　　Were impotent and vain

Whether the wretched mortal there
　　His filial hands imbrued,
Or if the ruler of the sky
　　The scene with pity view'd—

And sent the streaming bolt of heaven,
　　Ordained to interpose,
To take her life, and save her soul,
　　From these infernal foes,

No man can tell, how it befell ;
　　Inquiry all was vain ;
But thence she never more returned,
　　She there that night was slain.

And Willie Wilkin's noble steed
　　Lay stiff upon the green.
A night so dire in Annandale
　　Before had never been !

Loud thunders shook the vault of heaven,
  The bolts with fury flew;
The graves were plough'd, the rocks were riven;
  Whole flocks and herds it slew.

They gather'd up her mangled limbs,
  And laid beneath a stone ;
But heart, and tongue, and every palm
  From every hand were gone.

Her brains were dash'd against the wall,
  Her blood upon the floor;
Her reverend head, with sorrows gray,
  Hung on the chapel door.

To Auchincastle Wilkin hied,
  On Evan braes so green;
And liv'd and died like other men,
  For aught that could be seen.

But gloomy, gloomy was his look;
  And froward was his way;
And malice every action rul'd
  Until his dying day.

And many a mermaid staid his call,
  And many a mettled fay;
And many a wayward spirit learn'd
  His summons to obey.

And many a wondrous work he wrought,
And many things foretold;
Much was he fear'd but little loved,
By either young or old.

———

NOTES TO WILLIE WILKIN.

—

NOTE I.

He hied him to yon ancient fane
That stands by Kinnel side.

P. 83, v. 2.

The name of this ancient fane is Dumgree. It is
beautifully situated on the west side of the Kinnel, one
of the rivers which joins the Annan from the west, and
is now in ruins. It is still frequented by a few peaceable
spirits at certain seasons. As an instance: Not many
years ago, a neighbouring farmer, riding home at night
upon a mare, who, besides knowing the road well
enough, had her foal closed in at home, thought himself
hard at his own house, but was surprised to find that
his mare was stopped at the door of the old kirk of
Dumgree. He mounted again, and essayed it a second
and a third time; but always, when he thought himself

at home, he found himself at the door of the old church
of Dumgree, and farther from home than when he first
set out. He was now sensible that the beast was led
by some invisible hand, so alighting, he went into the
chapel and said his prayers; after which, he mounted,
and rode as straight home as if it had be 'n noon.

NOTE II.

To Auchincastle Wilkin hied
    On Evan braes so green.

P. 90, v.4.

Auchincastle is situated on the west side of the Evan,
another of the tributary streams of the Annan. It
seems to have been a place of great strength and anti-
quity; is surrounded by a moat and a fosse, and is,
perhaps, surpassed by none in Scotland for magnitude.

NOTE III.

And lived and died like other men,
    For aught that could be seen.

P. 90, v. 4.

If he lived and died like other men, it appears that
he was not at all buried like other men. When on his
death-bed, he charged his sons, as they valued their
peace and prosperity, to sing no requiem, nor say any
burial-service over his body; but to put a strong
withie to each end of his coffin, by which they were
to carry him away to Dumgree, and see that all the

attendants were well mounted. On the top of a certain eminence they were to set down the corpse and rest a few minutes, and if nothing interfered they might proceed. If they fulfilled these, he promised them the greatest happiness and prosperity for four generations; but, if they neglected them in one point, the utmost misery and wretchedness. The lads performed every thing according to their father's directions; and they had scarcely well set down the corpse on the place he mentioned, when they were alarmed by the most horrible bellowing of bulls; and instantly two dreadful brindered ones appeared, roaring, and snuffing, and tossing up the earth with their horns and hoofs; on which the whole company turned and fled. When the bulls reached the coffin, they put each of them one of their horns into their respective withies, and ran off with the corpse, stretching their course straight to the westward. The relatives, and such as were well mounted, pursued them, and kept nigh them for several miles; but when they came to the small water of Bram, in Nithsdale, the bulls went straight through the air from the one hill head to the other, without descending to the bottom of the glen. This unexpected manœuvre threw the pursuers quite behind, though they need not have expected any thing else, having before observed, that their feet left no traces on the ground, though ever so soft. However, by dint of whip and spur, they again got sight of them; but when they came to Loch Ettrick, on the heights of Closeburn, they had all lost sight of them but two, who were far behind: but the bulls there meeting with another company, plunged into the lake with the corpse, and were never more seen at that time. Ever

since, his spirit has haunted that loch, and continues
to do so to this day.

He was, when alive, very fond of the game of curl-
ing on the ice, at which no mortal man could beat
him; nor has his passion for it ceased with death; for
he and his hellish confederates continue to amuse
themselves with this game during the long winter
nights, to the great terror and annoyance of the
neighbourhood, not much regarding whether the loch
be frozen or not.

THIRLESTANE.

A FRAGMENT.

————

SIR ROBERT SCOTT, knight of Thirlestane, was first married to a lady of high birth and qualifications, whom he most tenderly loved; but she, soon dying, left him an only son. He was afterwards married to a lady of a different temper, by whom he had several children; whose jealousy of the heir made Sir Robert doat still more on this darling son. She, knowing that the right of inheritance belonged to him, and that, of course, a very small share would fall to her sons, seeing he loved the heir so tenderly, grew every year more uneasy. But the building, and other preparations which were going on at Gamescleuch, on the other side of the Ettrick, for his accommodation on reaching his majority, when he was also to be married to a fair kinswoman, drove her past all patience, and made her resolve on his destruction. The masonry of his new castle of Gamescleuch was finished on his birth-day, when he reached his twentieth year, but it never went farther. This being always a feast-day at Thirlestane, the lady prepared, on that day, to put her hellish plot in execution; for which purpose, she had previously secured to her interest John Lally, the family piper. This man, tradition says, procured her three adders, of which they chose the parts replete with most deadly poison; these they ground to a fine powder, and mixed with a bottle of wine. On the forenoon before the festival commenced, he went over to Gamescleuch to regale his workmen, who had exerted themselves to get their work finished on that day, and Lally the piper went with him as server. When his young lord called for wine to drink a health to the masons, John gave him a cup of the poisoned bottle, which he drank off. Lally went out of the castle, as if about to return home; but that was the last sight of him. He could never be found, nor heard of, though the most diligent and extended search was made for him. The heir swelled and burst almost instantaneously. A large company of the then potent name of Scott, with others, were now assembled at Thirlestane to grace the festival; but what a woeful meeting it turned out to be! They with one voice pronounced him poisoned; but where to attach the blame remained a mystery, as he was so universally loved and esteemed. The first thing the knight caused to be done, was blowing the blast on the trumpet or great bugle, which was the warning for all the family instantly to assemble, which they did in the court of the castle He then put the following question: "Now, are we all here? A voice answered from the crowd, "We are all here but Lally the piper." Simple and natural as the answer may seem, it served as an electrical shock to old Sir Robert. It is supposed that, knowing the confidence which his lady placed in this menial, the whole scene of cruelty opened to his eyes at once; and the trying conviction, that his peace was destroyed by her most dear to him, struck so forcibly upon his feelings, that it totally deprived him of reason. He stood a long time speechless, and then fell to repeating the answer which he received, like one half awakened out of a sleep; nor was he ever heard, for many a day, to speak another word than these, "We are all here but Lally the piper:" and when any one accosted him, whatever was the subject, that was sure to be the answer he received.

The method which he took to revenge his son's death was singular and unwarrantable: He said, that the estate of right belonged to his son, and since he could not bestow it upon him living, he would spend it all upon him now he was dead: and that neither the lady nor her children should ever enjoy a farthing of that which she had played so foully for. The body was accordingly embalmed, and lay in great splendour at Thirlestane for a year and a day; during all which time Sir Robert kept open house, welcoming and feasting all who chose to come, and actually spent or mortgaged his whole estate, saving a very small patrimony in Eskdale-muir, which belonged to his wife. Some say, that while all the country who chose to come were thus feasting at Thirlestane, she remained shut up in a vault of the castle, and lived on bread and water.

During the last three days of this wonderful feast, the crowds which gathered were immense; it seemed as if the whole country were assembled at Thirlestane. The butts of wine were carried to the open fields, the ends knocked out of them with hatchets, stones, or whatever came readiest to hand, and the liquor carried about "in stoups and in caups." On these days the burn of Thirlestane ran constantly red with wine, and even communicated its tincture to the river Ett-

7

rick. The family vault, where his corpse was interred
in a leaden chest, is under the same roof with the
present parish church of Ettrick, and distant from
Thirlestane about a Scots mile. To give some idea
of the magnitude of the burial, the old people tell us,
that though the whole way was crowded with attendants, yet, when the leaders of the procession reached
the church, the rearmost were not nearly got from
Thirlestane.

Sir Robert, shortly after dying, left his family in a
state little short of downright beggary, which, they
say, the lady herself came to before she died. As Sir
Robert's first lady was of the family of Harden, some
suspected him of having a share in forwarding the
knight's desperate procedure. Certain it is, however,
he did not, in this instance, depart from the old family
maxim, "Keep what you have, and catch what you
can," but made a noble hand of the mania of grief
which so overpowered the faculties of the old baron;
for when accounts came to be cleared up, a large pro-
portion of the lands turned out to be Harden's. And
it is added, on what authority I know not, that when
the extravagance of Sir William Scott obliged the
Harden family to part with these lands, the purchasers
were bound, by the bargain, to refund these lands,
should the Scotts of Thirlestane ever make good their
right to them, either by law or redemption.

The nearest lineal descendant from this second
marriage is one Robert Scott, a poor man who lives at
the Binks on Teviot, whom the generous Buccleuch
has taken notice of and provided for. He is commonly
distinguished by the appellation of *Rab the Laird*, from
the conviction of what he would have been had he

got fair play. With this man, who is very intelligent, I could never find an opportunity of conversing, though I sought it diligently. It is said, he can inform as to many particulars relating to this sad catastrophe; and that, whenever he has occasion to mention a certain great predecessor of his, (the lady of Thirlestane) he distinguishes her by the uncouth epithet of the d——d b——h. It must be remarked, that I had access to no records for the purpose of ascertaining the facts above stated, though I believe they are for the most part pretty correct. Perhaps much might be learned by applying to the noble representative of the family, the Honourable Lord Napier who is still possessed of the beautiful mountains round Thirlestane, and who has it at present in contemplation to rebuild and beautify it; which may God grant him health and prosperity to accomplish.—It is to this story that the following fragment relates.

THIRLESTANE.

A FRAGMENT.

———

FER, fer hee raide, and fer hee gaed,
    And aft he sailit the sea;
And thrise he crossit the Alpyne hills
    To distant Italie.

Beyon Lough-Ness his tempil stude,
    Ane ril of meikle fame;
A knight of gude Seant John's hee was,
    And Baldwin was his name.

By wondrous lore hee did explore
    What after tymes wald bee;
And manie mystic links of fate
    He hafflins culd fursee.

Fer, fer hee raide, and fer hee gaed,
    Owr mony hill and dale;
Till, passing through the fair foreste,
    He learnit a waesom tale.

Wher Ettrick wandirs down a plain,
 With lofty hills belay't,
The staitly towirs of Thirlestane
 With wunder hee surveyt.

Black hung the bannir on the wall;
 The trumpit seimit to grane;
And reid, reid ran the bonny burn,
 Whilk erst like siller shone.

At first a noise like fairie soundis
 He indistinctly heard;
Then countless, countless were the crouds
 Whilke round the walls appeir'd.

Thousands of steids stood on the hill,
 Of sable trappings vaine!
And round on Ettrick's baittle haughs
 Grew no kin kind of graine.

Hee gazit, hee wonderit, sair hee fearit
 Sum recent tragedie;
At length he spyit ane woeful wight
 Gaun droopin on the ley.

His beard was silverit owr wi' eild:
 Pale was his cheek wae-worn;
His hayre was like the muirland wild
 On a December morn.

" Halle, revirent brither," Baldwin said,
   " Here, in this unco land,
A temple warrior greets thee well,
   And offers thee his hand.

" O tell me why the poepill murn ?
   Sure all is not for gude :
And why, why does the bonnie burn
   Rin reid wi' Christain blude ?"

Ald Beattie turnit and shuke his heid,
   While down fell mony a teir ;
" O wellcom, wellcom, sire," he said,
   " Ane waesum tale to heire :

" The gude Sir Robert's sonne and aire
   By creuel handis lyis slain ;
And all his wide domains, so fair,
   To ither lords ar gane.

" On sik ane youth as him they mourn,
   The sun did never shine ;—
Instead of Christain blude, the burn
   Rins reid wi' Renis wine.

" This is the sad returnin day
   He first beheld the light ;
This is the sad returnin day
   He fell by cruel spite.

" And on this day, with pomp and pride,
 From hence you'll see him borne ;
And his poor faither sad return
 Of landis and onuris shorne.

" Come to my littill chambir still,
 In yonder turret low ;
We'll say our praiers for the dead,
 And for the leeving too.

" And when thou hast a free repast
 Of wheat bread and the wine,
My tale shall weet the onest cheeks,
 As oft it has dune mine."

  • • • • • •

LORD DERWENT.

A FRAGMENT.

"O why look ye so pale, my lord?
    And why look ye so wan?
And why stand mounted at your gate,
    So early in the dawn?"

"O well may I look pale, lady!
    For how can I look gay,
When I have fought the live-long night,
    And fled at break of day."

"And is the border troop arrived?
    And have they won the day?
It must have been a bloody field,
    Ere Derwent fled away.

"But where got ye that stately steed,
    So stable and so good?
And where got ye that gilded sword,
    So dyed with purple blood?"

" I got that sword in bloody fray,
  Last night on Eden downe ;
I got the horse, and harness too,
  Where mortal ne'er got one."

" Alight, alight, my noble lord;
  God mot you save and see ;
For never, till this hour, was I
  Afraid to look on thee."

He turned him to the glowing east,
  That stained both tower and tree :
" Prepare, prepare, my lady fair,
  Prepare to follow me.

" Before this dawning day shall close,
  A deed shall here be done,
That men unborn shall shrink to hear,
  And dames the tale shall shun.

" The conscious morning blushes deep,
  The foul intent to see.
Prepare, prepare, my lady fair,
  Prepare to follow me."

" Alight, alight, my noble lord,
  I'll live or die with thee ;
I see a wound deep in your side,
  And hence you cannot flee."

She looked out o'er her left shoulder
   To list a heavy groan ;
But when she turned her round again,
   Her noble lord was gone.

She looked to east, and west, and south,
   And all around the tower ;
Through house and hall, but man nor horse
   She never could see more.

She turned her round, and round about,
   All in a doleful state ;
And there she saw her little foot page
   Alighting at the gate.

" O ! open, open, noble dame,
   And let your servant in ;
Our furious foes are hard at hand,
   The castle fair to win."

" But tell me, Billy, where's my lord ?
   Or whither is he bound ?
He's gone just now, and in his side
   A deep and deadly wound."

" Why do you rave, my noble dame,
   And look so wild on me ?
Your lord lies on the bloody field,
   And him you'll never see.

" With Scottish Jardine, hand to hand,
    He fought most valiantly,
Put him to flight, and broke his men,
    With shouts of victory.

"But Maxwell rallying, wheeled about,
    And charged as fierce as hell;
Yet ne'er could pierce the English troop
    Till my brave master fell.

" Then all was gone; the ruffian Scot
    Bore down our flying band;
And now they waste, with fire and sword,
    The Links of Cumberland.

"Lord Maxwell's gone to Carlisle town,
    With Jardine bold and true;
And young Kilpatrick and Glencairn
    Are come in search of you."

" How dare you lie, my little page,
    Whom I pay meat and fee ?
The cock has never crowed but once
    Since Derwent was with me.

" The bird that sits on yonder bush,
    And sings so loud and clear,
Has only three times changed his note
    Since my good lord was here."

" Whoe'er it was, whate'er it was,
 I'm sure it was not he:
I saw him slain on Eden plain,
 And him you'll never see.

" I saw him stand against a host,
 While heaps before him fell:
I saw them pierce his manly side,
 And bring his last farewell.

" O run! he cried, to my ladye.
 And bear the fray before;
Tell her I died for England's right—
 Then word spake never more.

" Come, let us fly to Westmoreland,
 For here you cannot stay;
We'll fairly shift; our steeds are swift;
 And well I know the way."

" I will not fly, I cannot fly,
 My heart is wonder sore;
My brain it turns, my blood it burns,
 And all with me is o'er."

She turned her eyes to Borrowdale;
 Her heart grew chill with dread—
For there she saw the Scottish band,
 Kilpatrick at their head.

Red blazed the beacon on Pownell;
  On Skiddaw there were three;
The warder's horn, on muir and fell,
  Was heard continually.

Dark grew the sky, the wind was still,
  The sun in blood arose;
But oh! how many a gallant man
  Ne'er saw that evening close!

* * * * * *

NOTES TO LORD DERWENT.

—

NOTE 1.

I got that sword in bloody fray,
  Last night on Eden downe.

P. 106. v. 1.

This ballad relates to an engagement which took place betwixt the Scots and English, in Cumberland, A. D. 1524; for a particular account of which, see the historians of that time.

NOTE II

But Maxwell rallying, wheeled about.

P. 108. v. 2.

The page's account of this action seems not to be wide of the truth: "On the 17th of Julie, the Lord Maxwell, and Sir Alexander Jardein with diverse other Scottishmen, in great numbers, entered England by the west marches and Caerleill, with displayed banners, and began to harrie the country, and burn diverse places. The Englishmen assembled on every side, so that they were far more in number than the Scottishmen, and thereupon set feircelie upon their enemies: insomuch, that, for the space of an hour, there was a sore fight continued betwixt them. But the Lord Maxwell, like a true politike captain, as of all that knew him he was no less reputed, ceased not to encourage his people; and after that, by the taking of Sir Alexander Jardein and others, they had beene put backe, he brought them in arraie again, and, beginning a new skirmish, recovered in manner all the prisoners; took and slew diverse Englishmen; so that he returned with victorie, and led above 300 prisoners with him into Scotland.' —HOLINSHED.

THE
LAIRD OF LAIRISTAN,

OR, THE

THREE CHAMPIONS OF LIDDISDALE.

The scene of this ballad is laid in the upper parts of Liddisdale, in which district the several residencies of the three champions are situated, as is also the old castle of Hermitage, with the farm-houses of Saughentree and Roughley. As to the authenticity of the story, all that I can say of it is, that I used to hear it told when I was a boy, by William Scott, a joiner of that country, and was much taken with some of the circumstances. Were I to relate it verbatim, it would only be anticipating a great share of the poem.—One verse is ancient, beginning, O wae be to thee, &c.

"O WILLIE, 'tis light, and the moon shines bright,
    Will ye go and watch the deer wi' me ?"
"Ay, be my sooth, this very night :"
    And away they went to the Saughentree.

The moon had turn'd the roof of heaven;
　The ground lay deep in drifted snaw;
The hermitage bell had rung eleven,
　When lo! a wondrous sight they saw.

Right owr the knowe where Liddel lyes—
　Nae wonder that it catch'd his ee!
A thing of huge and monstrous size
　Was steering that way hastilye.

"Ah! what is yon, my brother John?
　Now God preserve baith you and me!
But our guns they are load, and what comes in
　　　　their road,
　Be't boggle, or robber, these bullets shall prie."

"O haud your tongue, my brother dear;
　Let us survey't with steedy ee;
'Tis surely a man they are carrying here,
　And 'tis fit that the family warn'd should be."

They ran to the ha', and they waken'd them a',
　Where none where at home but maidens three;
And into the shade of the wall they have staid,
　To watch what the issue of this would be.

And there they saw a dismal sight!
　A sight had nearly freez'd their blood!
One lost her reason that very night,
　And one of them fainted where they stood.

Four stalwart men, on arms so bright,
   Came bearing a corpse with many a wound;
His habit bespoke him a lord or knight;
   And his fair ringlets swept the ground.

They heard a voice to the other say—
   " A place to leave him will not be found;
The barn is lock'd, and the key away."—
   Said one, "In the byre we'll lay him down."

Then into the byre the corpse they bore,
   And away they fled right speedilye;
The rest took shelter within the door,
   In wild amazement, as well might be.

And into the byre no ane durst gang,
   No, not for the life of his bodye;
But the blood on the snaw was trailed alang,
   And the kend a' wasna as it should be

Next morning all the Dalesmen ran;
   For soon the word was far and wide;
And there lay the Laird of Lairistan,
   The bravest knight on the border side!

He was wounded behind, and wounded before,
   And cloven through the left cheek-bone;
And clad in the habit he daily wore;
   But his sword, and his belt, and his bonnet were
      gone.

Then east and west the word has gane,
   And soon to Branxholm ha' it flew,
That Elliot of Lairistan he was slain,
   But how or why no creature knew.

Buccleugh has mounted his milk-white steed,
   With fifteen knights in his companye;
To Hermitage Castle they rode with speed,
   Where all the dale was summon'd to be.

And soon they came, a numerous host,
   And they swore, and touch'd the dead bodie;
But Jocky o' Millburn he was lost,
   And could not be found in the hale countrye.

" Now, wae be to thee, Armstrong o' Millburn!
   And O an ill death may'st thou dee!
Through thee we have lost brave Lairistan,
   But his equal thou wilt never be.

" The Bewcastle men may ramp and rave,
   And drive away the Liddisdale kye:
For now is our guardian laid in his grave;
   And Branxholm and Thirlestane distant lye.

The Dales-men thus his loss deplore,
   And every one his virtues tell:
His hounds lay howling at the door;
   His hawks flew idle o'er the fell.

When three long years were come and gone,
   Two shepherds sat on Roughly hill;
And ay they sigh'd, and made their moan,
   O'er present times that look'd so ill.

" Our young king lives at London town,
   Buccleuch must bear him companye;
And Thirlestane's all to ruin gone,
   And who shall our protector be?

" And jealous of the Stuart race,
   The English lords began to thraw;
The land is in a piteous case,
   When subjects rise against the law.

" Ere all is done, our blood may soak
   Our Scottish houms, and leave a stain—
A stain like that on Sundup's cloak,
   Which never will wash out again."

Amazement kyth'd in Sandy's face
   His mouth to open wide began;
He star'd, and look'd from place to place,
   As events o'er his mem'ry ran.

The broider'd cloak of gaudy green
   That Sundup wore, and was sae gay,
For three lang years had ne'er been seen,
   At chapel, raid, nor holidav

He minded too, he once o'erheard,
   (When courting of his bonny Ann)
A hint, the which he greatly fear'd,
   But ne'er could thoroughly understand.

" Now tell me, Willie, tell me true ;
   Your sim'lie bodes us little good ;
I fear the cloak you mention'd now—
   I fear 'tis stain'd with noble blood!"

" Indeed, my friend, you've guess'd aright ;
   I never meant to tell to man
That tale : but crimes will come to light,
   Let human wits do what they can.

" But He, who ruleth wise and well,
   Hath ordered from his seat on high,
That ay since valiant Elliot fell
   This mantle bears the purple dye.

" And all the waters in Liddisdale,
   And all that lash the British shore.
Can ne'er wash out the wondrous maele !
   It still seems fresh with purple gore."

Then east and west the word has gane,
   And soon to Branxholm hall it flew ;
And Halbert o' Sundup hee was ta'en,
   And brought before the high Buccleuch.

The cloak was hung in open hall,
    Where ladies and lords of high degree,
And many a one, both great and small,
    Were struck with awe the same to see.

"Now tell me, Sundup," said Buccleuch,
    "If this is rul'd by God on high?
If that is Elliot's blood we view,
    False Sundup! thou shalt surely die."

Then Halbert turn'd him where he stood,
    And wip'd the round tear from his ee;
"That blood, my lord is, Elliot's blood;
    I winna keep the truth frae thee."

"O ever-alack!" said good Buccleuch,
    "If that be true thou tell'st to me,
On the highest tree in Branxholm heuch.
    Stout Sundup, thou must hangit be."

"'Tis Elliot's blood; I tell you true:
    And Elliot's death was wrought by me;
And were the deed again to do,
    I'd do't in spite of hell and thee.

"My sister, brave Jock Armstrong's bride,
    The fairest flower of Liddisdale,
By Elliot basely was betray'd;
    And roundly has he paid the mail.

" We watch'd him in her secret bower,
　And found her to his bosom prest ;
He begged to have his broad claymore,
　And dar'd us both to do our best.

" Perhaps, my lord, ye'll truly say,
　In rage, from laws of arms we swerv'd
Though Lairistan got double play,
　'Twas fairer play than he deserv'd.

" We might have kill'd him in the dark,
　When in the lady's arms lay he ;
We might have killed him in his sark,
　Yet gave him room to fight or flee.

" Come on, then, gallant Milburn cry'd,
　My single arm shall do the deed ;
Or heavenly justice is denied,
　Or that false heart of thine shall bleed.

" Then to't they fell, both sharp and snell,
　With steady hand and watchful eye ;
Soon blood and sweat from either fell ;
　And from their swords the sparkles fly.

" The first stroke Milburn to him wan,
　He ript his bosom to the bone ;
Though Armstrong was a gallant man,
　Like Elliot living there was none.

"His growth was like the border oak;
  His strength the bison's strength outvied;
His courage like the mountain rock;
  For skill his man he never tried.

"Oft had we three, in Border fray,
  Made chiefs and armies stand in awe;
And little thought to see the day,
  On other deadly thus to draw.

"The first wound that brave Milburn got,
  The tear of rage row'd in his ee;
The next stroke that brave Milburn got,
  The blood ran dreeping to his knee.

"My sword I grip'd into my hand,
  And fast to his assistance ran;
What could I do? I could not stand,
  And see the base deceiver win.

"O turn thee, turn thee, limmer loun!
  O turn and change a blow with me,
Or, by the righteous powèrs aboon,
  I'll hew the arm from thy bodye.

"He turn'd with many a haughty word,
  And lounged and struck most furiouslye;

But with one slap of my broad sword
  I brought the traitor to his knee.

"Now take thou that, stout Armstrong cry'd,
  For all the pains thou'st gi'en to me;
(Though then he shortly would have died)
  And ran him through the fair bodye."

———

Buccleuch's stern look began to change;
  To tine a warrior loath was he;
The crime was called a brave revenge,
  And Halbert of Sundup was set free.

Then every man for Milburn mourn'd,
  And wish'd him to enjoy his own;
But Milburn never more return'd
  Till ten long years were come and gone.

Then loud alarms through England ring,
  And deeds of death and dool began;
The commons rose against the king,
  And friends to diff'rent parties ran.

The nobles join the royal train,
   And soon his ranks with grandeur fill;
They sought their foes with might and main,
   And found them lying on Edgehill.

The trumpets blew, the bullets flew,
   And long and bloody was the fray;
At length o'erpower'd, the rebel crew
   Before the royal troops gave way.

"Who was the man," Lord Lindsey cry'd,
   "That fought so well through all the fray
Whose coat of rags, together ty'd,
   Seems to have seen a better day!

"Such bravery in so poor array,
   I never in my life did see;
His valour three times turn'd the day.
   When we were on the point to flee."

Then up there spoke a man of note,
   Who stood beside his majestie,
"My liege, the man's a border Scot,
   Who volunteer'd to fight for thee."

The king he smil'd, and said aloud,
   "Go bring the valiant Scot to me;
When we have all our foes subdued,
   The Lord of Liddil he shall be."

The king gave him his gay gold ring,
   And made him there a belted knight;
But Milburn bled to save his king!
   The king to save his royal right!

SANDY TOD.

A SCOTTISH PASTORAL.

TO A LADY.

You ha'e learned in love to languish,
   You ha'e felt affliction's rod,
Murn wi' me the meltin' anguish,
   Murn the loss o' Sandy Tod.

Sandy was a lad o' vigour,
   Clean an' tight o' lith an' lim'.
For a decent, manly figure,
   Few cou'd ding or equal him.

In a cottage, poor and nameless,
   By a little bouzy linn,
Sandy led a life so blameless,
   Far frae ony strife or din.

125

Annan's fertile dale beyon' him,
  Spread her fields an' meadows green;
Hoary Hertfell towered aboon him,
  Smilin' to the sun—gude e'en.

Few his wants, his wishes fewer,
  Save his flocks nae care had he;
Never heart than his was truer,
  Tender to the last degree.

He was learned, and every tittle
  E'er he read believed it true;
Savin' chapters cross an' kittle,
  He cou'd read his bible through.

Oft he read the acts o' Joseph,
  How wi' a' his friends he met;
Ay the hair his noddle rose off,
  Ay his cheeks wi' tears were wet.

Seven bonny buskit simmers
  O'er the Solway Frith had fled,
Since a flock o' ewes an' gimmers
  Out amang the hills he fed.

Some might bragg o' knowledge deeper,
  But nae herd was lo'ed sae weel;
Sandy's hirsel proved their keeper
  Was a cannie carefu' chiel'.

Ay when ony tentless lammie
  Wi' its neibours chanced to go,
Sandy kend the careless mammy,
  Whether she cried *mae* or no.

Warldly walth an' grandeur scornin',
  Peace adorned his little bield;
Ilka e'enin', ilka mornin',
  Sandy to his Maker kneeled.

You wha roun' wi' diamonds wrap ye,
  An' are fanned wi' loud applause,
Can ye trou the lad was happy?
  Really 'tis believed he was.

In the day sae black an' showery,
  I ha'e seen the bonny bow,
When arrayed in all its glory,
  Vanish on the mountain's brow.

Sae ha'e ye, my lovely marrow,
  Seen the rose an' vi'let blue,
Bloomin' on the banks of Yarrow,
  Quickly fade, an' lose their hue;

Fadin' as the forest roses,
  Transient as the radiant bow,
Fleetin' as the shower that follows,
  Is our happiness below.

Unadmired she'll hover near ye,
  In the rural sport she'll play;
Woo her—she'll at distance hear ye,
  Press her—she is gane for ay.

She had Sandy ay attendit,
  Seemed obedient to his nod;
Now his happy hours are endit,
  Lack-a-day for Sandy Tod.

I' the kirk ae Sunday sittin',
  Whar to be he seldom failed,
Sandy's tender heart was smitten
  Wi' a wound that never healed;

Sally, dressed i' hat an' feather,
  Placed her in a neibrin' pew,
Sandy sat—he kendna whether!
  Sandy felt—he wistna how.

Though the priest alarmed the audience,
  An' drew tears frae mony een,
Sandy heard a noise like baudrons
  Murrin' i' the bed at e'en!

Aince or twice his sin alarmed him,
  Down he looked, an' wished a prayer;
Sally had o' sense disarmed him,
  Heart an' mind an' a' was there!

Luckily her een were from him ;
   Ay they beamed anither road ;
Aince a smilin' glance set on him—
   " Mercy, Lord !" quo' Sandy Tod.

A' that night he lay an' turned him,
   Fastit a' the followin' day ;
Now the eastern lamps war burnin',
   Westward fled the gloomin' gray.

Res'lute made by desperation,
   Down the glen in haste he flew,
Quickly reached the habitation
   Where his sweet carnation grew.

I wad sing the happy meetin',
   War it new or strange to thee ;
Weel ye ken 'tis but repeatin'
   What has past 'tween you and me.

Thy white hand around me pressed,
   My unresty heart has felt ;
But, whan hers on Sandy rested,
   His fond heart was like to melt !

Lockit to his bosom duntin'
   Listless a' the night she lay,
Orion's belt had bored the mountain,
   Loud the cock had crawed the day.

9

Sandy rase—his bonnet daddit—
　Begged a kiss—gat nine or ten;
Then the hay, sae ruffed an' saddit,
　Towzlet up that nane might ken.

You ha'e seen, on April mornin',
　Light o' heart, the pretty lamb
Skippin', dancin', bondage scornin',
　Wander heedless o' its dam?

Sometimes gaun, an' sometimes rinnin',
　Sandy to his mountains ran;
Roun' aboon his flocks gaed singin',
　Never was a blyther man;

Never did his native nation,
　Sun or sky, wear sic a hue;
In his een the hale creation
　Wore a face entirely new.

Weel he lo'ed his faithfu' Ruffler,
　Weel the bird sang on the tree;
Meanest creatures doomed to suffer,
　Brought the tear into his ee.

Sandy's heart was undesignin',
　Soft and lovin' as the dove;
Scarcely cou'd it bear refinin'
　By the gentle fire o' love.

You ha'e seen the cunnin' fowler
   Wile the airy bird to death;
Blossoms nipt by breezes fouler,
   Or by winter's wastin' breath?

Sally's blossom soon was blighted
   By untimely winter prest;
Sally had been woed an' slighted
   By a farmer in the west.

Sandy daily lo'ed her dearer,
   Kendna she afore was won,
Aince, whan he gaed down to see her,
   Sally had a dainty son!

Sternies, blush an' hide your faces;
   Veil the moon in sable hue;
Else thy locks, for human vices,
   Soon will dreep wi' pity's dew!

Thou who rules the rolling thunder,
   Thou who darts the flying flame,
Wilt thou vengeance ay keep under
   Due for injured love an' fame?

Cease, my charmer, cease bewailin',
   Down thy cheeks the pearls do shine;
Cease to mourn thy sex's failin',
   I maun drop a tear for mine:

Man, the lord o' the creation,
   Lighten'd wi' a ray divine,
Lost to feelin', truth, an' caution,
   Lags the brutal tribes behind !

You ha'e seen the harmless conie
   Following hame its mate to rest ;
One ensnared, the frighted cronie
   Fled amazed wi' pantin' breast.

Petrified, an' dumb wi' horror,
   Sandy fled, he kendna where ,
Never heart than his was sorer,
   It was mair than he cou'd bear !

Seven days on yonder mountain
   Lay he sobbin', late an' soon,
Till discovered by a fountain,
   Railin' at the dowy moon.

Weepin' a' the day, he'd wander
   Through yon dismal glen alane ;
By the stream at night wad dander,
   Ravin' owr his Sally's name

Shun'd an' pitied by the world,
   Long a humblin' sight was he,
Till that fatal moment hurled
   Him to lang eternity.

Sittin' on yon cliff sae rocky,
　Fearless as the boding crow—
No, my dear, I winna shock ye
　Wi' the bloody scene below.

By yon aek, decayed an' rottin',
　Where the hardy woodbin' twines,
Now, in peace, he sleeps forgotten;
　Owr his head these simple lines:—

"Lovers, pause, while I implore ye
　Still to walk in virtue's road;
An' to say, when ye gang o'er me,
　Lack-a-day, for Sandy Tod!"

FAREWELL TO ETTRICK.

—

FAREWEEL, my Ettrick ! fare-ye-weel !
  I own I'm unco laith to leave ye ;
Nane kens the half o' what I feel,
  Nor half the cause I ha'e to grieve me !

There first I saw the rising morn ;
  The first my infant mind unfurl'd,
To judge that spot where I was born
  The very centre o' the world !

I thought the hills were sharp as knives,
  An' the braed lift lay whomel'd on them,
An' glowr'd wi' wonder at the wives
  That spak o' ither hills ayon' them.

When ilka year ga'e something new,
  Addition to my mind or stature,
As fast my love for Ettrick grew,
  Implanted in my very nature.

134

I've sung, in mony a rustic lay,
　　Her heroes, an' her hills sae green ;
Her woods and vallies fresh and gay ;
　　Her honest lads and lasses clean.

I had a thought—a poor vain thought !
　　I thought that I might do her honour;
But a' my hopes are come to nought,
　　I'm forc'd to turn my back upon her !

She's thrown me out o' house an' hauld !
　　My heart got never sic a thrust !
An' my poor parents, frail an' auld,
　　Are forc'd to leave their kindred dust !

But fare-ye-weel, my native streams,
　　Frae a' sic dule be ye preserv'd :
Ye'll find ye cherish some at hame
　　That disna just sae weel deserv't.

There is nae man on a' your banks
　　Will ever say that I did wrang him
The lasses ha'e my dearest thanks
　　For a' the joys I had amang them.

Though twin'd by rough an' ragin' seas,
　　An' risin' hills an' rollin' rivers :
To think o' them I'll never cease,
　　Until my heart ga'e a' to shivers !

I'll make the Harris rocks to ring
    Wi' ditties wild, when nane shall hear;
The Lewis shores shall learn to sing
    The names o' them I lo'ed so dear.

My Peggy's ay aboon the lave,
    I'll carve on ilka lonely green;
The sea-bird, tossin' on the wave,
    Shall learn the name o' bonny Jean.

Ye gods, tak' care o' my dear lass!
    That as I leave her I may find her;
Till that blest time shall come to pass
    We'll meet again, and never sinder.

Fareweel, my Ettrick! fare-ye-weel!
    I own I'm unco wae to leave ye;
Nane kens the half o' what I feel,
    Nor half o' that I ha'e to grieve me!

My parents, crazy grown wi' eild,
    How I rejoic'd to be their stay;
I thought to stand their help an' shield,
    Until an' at their latest day.

Wi' gentle hand to close their een,
    An' weet the yerd wi' mony a tear,
That held the dust o' ilka frien';
    O' friens so tender an' sincere!

It winna do ;—I maun away
  To yon rough isle sae bleak an' dun ;
Lang will they mourn, baith night an' day,
  The absence o' their darlin' son.

An' my dear Will ! how will I fen'
  Without thy kind an' ardent care !
Without thy verse-inspirin' pen,
  My muse will sleep an' sing nae mair.

Fareweel to a' my kith an' kin !
  To ilka frien' I held sae dear '
How happy often ha'e we been,
  Wi' music, mirth, an' welcome cheer :

Nae mair your gilded banks at noon,
  An answer to my flute will swell !
Nae mair the viol sweet I'll tune,
  That a' the younkers lo'ed sae well !

Nae mair amang the hags an' rocks,
  While hounds wi' music filled the air,
We'll hunt the sly an' cruel fox,
  Or trace the warie, circlin' hare !

My happy days wi' you are past ;
  An' waes my heart ! will ne'er return !
The brightest day will overcast !
  An' man was made at times to mourn.

But if I kend my dyin' day,
  Though distant, weary, pale, an' wan.
I'd tak my staff an' post away
  To yield my life where it began.

If in yon lone sequester'd place
  The tyrant Death should lay me low,
Oh! drap a tear, an' say—Alas!
  For him who lov'd an' honour'd you.

Fareweel, my Ettrick! fare-ye-weel,
  I own I'm something wae to leave ye!
Nane kens the half o' what I feel!
  Nor half the cause I ha'e to grieve me!

EPISTLE

TO MR. T. M. C., LONDON.

PUBLISHED IN THE SCOT'S MAGAZINE.

————

My blessin' on you, T. M. C.,
Like you there are nae mony mae:
For mony a year, wi' eager een,
I've glowr'd owr Scotia's Magazine;
And oft, like zealots at a sermon,
Discoverin' beauties whar there were none;
But never a' my life, till now,
Have I met sic a chiel' as you;
Sae sly, sae shrewd, sae queer a creature,
Sae weel aquaint wi' simple nature,
Sae gay, sae easy, an' sae ranty,
Sae cappernaity, an' sae canty:
For when I sing your songs sae gay,
To lasses at the bught or hay,
They blush, an' smurtlin, own they like them,
The thoughts they thought afore sae strikes
    them.
  Whether 'tis from a similarity
Of feelings, hitting to a rarity;

139

Or if in verse you soar away,
Far, far beyond my simple lay,
An' into nature tak' a stretch,
Whilk I wad fain, but canna reach;
Or if ae planet held the sway
When we were born I canna say;
But frae sic causes, or some other,
I feel a wish to ca' you brother.

 Then, Billy, set your foot to mine.
Let baith our buoyant brains combine
To raise our country's Magazine
Aboon the times that yet ha'e been.
Then tak' some pains to double rhyme,
Gar line wi' line keep equal time,
An' then, though critics back should fling us,
The de'ils shall dadd in vain to ding us.
Though Pegasus may be denied,
By lofty bards sae occupied,
Wi' joy we'll mount our cuddy asses,
An' scour like fire around Parnassus,
An' gather flowers of ilka hue,
To bind auld Scotland's honest brow
The upstarts new shall a' be snubbit,
And Ruddiman he sadly rubbit.

 How could ye leave our hoary hill?
Our ruggit rocks and rattling rills?
Our woodlands wild, an' waters mony?
Our lasses chaste, an' sweet, an' bonny?
The warrior's nurse, the poet's theme!
The seat of innocence an'—hame!

We've sic a short time here to fare,
'Tis little matter how or where ;
An' I wad chuse at least eleven
'Fore London, for the road to heaven.

   I neither ken your name nor bearin';*
Only I ken ye are a queer ane,
An' guess, for insight, wealth, or knowledge,
Ye've ta'en the desk, or musty college ;
To turn a pedant or translator,
And slight the genuine school of nature.
Sweet dame ! she met me single handed ;
Yet studying her, my mind expanded
To bounds are neither rack'd nor narrow,
On Ettrick banks an' braes of Yarrow.

   An' though your life should glide away
In pleasure's dear an' devious way,
Regret will sometimes pierce the heart,
An' leave a dour an' deadly smart,
An' when death comes, I'm wae for thee
Nae real friend to close your ee !
Or owr a son or brother's bier
To shed the sad regretfu' tear !
But just let down, wi' strings an' pullies,
To sleep wi' w——es, an' bucks, an' bullies ;

* The gentleman, to whom this epistle was addressed, is Mr. Thomas Mouncey Cunninghame, from Dumfries-shire, the author of many ingenious essays in the Scots Magazine ; but, at the writing of this, the author knew nothing of him.

An' when the summons reach the dead anes,
To rise in droves frae 'mang the headstanes,
Poor Tam may gang an' stand alane,
Of fellow faces he'll see nane,
But a' the croud gaun throu'ther, throu'ther,
Wi' ruefu' looks out owr ilk shouther.

O leave that lake of louns an' lechery,
Of folly, falsehood, tricks, and treachery;
Though oft a thriving place for low wits,
L—d, it's a dangerous place for poets!

If life's a blessing—'tween twa brothers,
The poor enjoy't as lang as others.
If health surpasses sumptuous fare,
Of that they ha'e their ample share.
What wad ye ha'e then? Dinna wrang us,
Come back an' live an' die amang us.
I lang to sing a sonnet wi' thee,
An' bonny Bessy sighs to see thee:
O! when she's sic a kind an' bonny ane,
Come—wed, an' turn a Cameronian.

While round our coast the ocean rows;
While on the Grampians heather grows;
While goud and gear the miser heaps up,
An' ill-will between cadgers keeps up;
While simple ease improves the feature,
An' best becomes the cheek o' nature;
As sterns the sky, and spots the leopard—
Count on

       Your friend,

          THE ETTRICK SHEPHERD.

THE

AUTHOR'S ADDRESS

TO HIS

AULD DOG HECTOR.

———

COME, my auld, towzy, trusty friend;
   What gars ye look sae douth an' wae?
D'ye think my favour's at an end,
   Because thy head is turnin' gray?

Although thy feet begin to fail,
   Their best were spent in serving me;
An' can I grudge thy wee bit meal,
   Some comfort in thy age to gi'e?

For mony a day, frae sun to sun,
   We've toil'd an' helpit ane anither;
An' mony a thousand mile thou'st run'
   To keep my thraward flocks the gither

143

To nae thrawn boy, nor scrawghin wife,
   Shall thy auld banes become a drudge;
At cats an' callans, a' thy life,
   Thou ever bore a mortal grudge.

An' whiles thy surly looks declared,
   Thou lo'ed the women warst of a';
'Cause aft they my affection shared,
   Which thou couldst never bruik at a'.

When sitting with my bonny Meg,
   Mair happy than a prince could be,
Thou plac'd thee by her other leg,
   An' watched her wi' a jealous ee.

An' then, at ony start or steer,
   Thou wad ha'e worried furiouslye;
While I was forc'd to curse and swear,
   Afore thou wad forbidden be.

Yet wad she clasp thy towzy paw;
   Thy greesome grips were never skaithly;
An' thou than her hast been mair true!
   An' truer than the friend that ga'e thee!

Ah, me! of fashion, health, an' pride,
   The world has read me sic a lecture!
But yet it's a' in part repaid
   By thee, my faithful, grateful Hector!

O'er past imprudence, oft alane
   I've shed the saut an' silent tear;
Then sharing ay my grief an' pain,
   My poor auld friend came snoovin' near.

For a' the days we've sojourned here,
   An they've been neither fine nor few,
That thought possest thee year to year,
   That a' my griefs arase frae you.

Wi' waesome face, and hingin' head,
   Thou wad ha'e press'd thee to my knee;
While I thy looks as weel could read,
   As thou hadst said in words to me—

" O my dear master, dinna greet;
   What ha'e I ever done to vex ye?
See here I'm cowrin' at your feet;
   Just take my life if I perplex ye.

" For a' my toil, my wee drap meat
   Is a' the wage I ask of thee;
For whilk I'm oft oblig'd to wait
   Wi' hungry wame, an' patient ee.

" Whatever wayward course ye steer;
   Whatever sad mischance o'ertake ye:
Man, here is ane will hald ye dear!
   Man, here's a friend will ne'er forsake ye!"

Yes, my puir beast! though friends me scorn,
  Whom mair than life I valued dear;
An' throw me out to fight forlorn,
  Wi' ills my heart dow hardly bear.

While I have thee to bear a part—
  My plaid, my health, an' heezle rung—
I'll scorn the silly haughty heart,
  The saucy look, and slanderous tongue.

Sure friends by pop'lar envy sway'd,
  Are ten times waur than ony fae!
My heart was theirs, an' to them laid
  As open as the light o' day.

I fear'd my aim; but never dredd
  That I for loss o' theirs should mourn;
Or that, when luck or favour fled,
  Their friendship wad injurious turn.

But He, who feeds the ravens young,
  Lets naething pass unheeded bye;
He'll sometime judge of right an' wrong,
  An' ay provide for you and I.

And hear me, Hector: thee I'll trust,
  As far as thou hast wit an' skill;
Sae will I ae sweet lovely breast,
  To me a balm for every ill.

To these my faith shall ever run,
   While I have reason truth to scan;
But ne'er, beyond my mother's son,
   To aught that bears the shape of man.—

I ne'er could thole thy cravin' face,
   Nor when ye pattit on my knee;
Though in a far an' unco place,
   I've whiles been forc'd to beg for thee.

Even now I'm in my master's power,
   Where my regard may scarce be shown;
But ere I'm forc'd to gi'e thee o'er,
   When thou art old an' useless grown,

I'll get a cottage o' my ain,
   Some wee bit cannie, lonely biel',
Where thy auld heart shall rest fu' fain,
   An' share with me my humble meal.

Thy post shall be to guard the door,
   An' bark at pethers, boys, an' whips;
Of cats an' hens to clear the floor,
   An' bite the flaes that vex thy hips.

When my last bannock's on the hearth,
   Of that thou sanna want thy share;
While I have house or hald on earth,
   My Hector shall ha'e shelter there.

An' should grim death thy noddle save,
   Till he has made an end of me ;
Ye'll lye a wee while on the grave
   Of ane wha ay was kind to thee.

There's nane alive will miss me mair ;
   An though in words thou canst not wail,
On a' the claes thy master ware,
   Thou'lt smell, and fawn, an' wag thy tail.

An' if I'm forc'd with thee to part,
   Which will be sair against my will ;
I'll sometimes mind thy honest heart,
   As lang as I can climb a hill.

Come, my auld, towzy, trusty tike,
   Let's speel away to Queensb'ry's lofty brow,
There greedy midges never fike !
   There care an' envy never grow.

While gazing down the fertile dales,
   Content an' peace shall ay be by ;
An' muses leave their native vales
   To rove at large wi' you and I.

THE

FOREST MINSTREL.

149

CLASS FIRST.

—

Pathetic Songs.

—

151

THE

FOREST MINSTREL.

THE SOLDIER'S WIDOW.

Tune—*Gilderoy*.

An' art thou fled, my bonny boy,
　An' left me here alane?
Wha now will love or care for me,
　When thou art dead an' gane?
Thy father fell in freedom's cause,
　With gallant Moore, in Spain:
Now thou art gane, my bonny boy,
　An' left me here alane.

I hop'd, when thou wert grown a man,
　To trae his looks in thine;
An' saw, wi' joy, thy sparkling eye
　Wi' kindling vigour shine.

153

I thought, when I was fail'd, I might
  Wi' you an' yours remain :
But thou art fled, my bonny boy,
  An' left me here alane.

Now clos'd an' set that sparkling eye !
  Thy breast is cauld as clay !
An' a' my hope, an' a' my joy,
  Wi' thee are reft away.
Ah ! fain wad I that comely clay
  Reanimate again !
But thou art fled, my bonny boy,
  An' left me here alane.

The flower, now fading on the lee,
  Shall fresher rise to view ;
The leaf, just fallen from the tree,
  The year will soon renew :
But lang may I weep o'er thy grave,
  Ere you revive again ;
For thou art fled, my bonny boy !
  An' left me here alane.

THE FLOWER.

O SOFTLY blow, thou biting blast,
  O'er Yarrow's lonely dale ;

And spare yon bonny tender bud
   Exposed to every gale;
Long has she hung her drooping head,
   Despairing to survive,
But transient sunbeams, through the cloud,
   Still kept my flower alive.

One sweetly scented summer eve
   To yonder bower I stray'd;
While little birds from ev'ry bough
   Their music wild convey'd.
The sunbeam lean'd across the shower;
   The rainbow girt the sky;
'Twas then I saw this lovely flower,
   An' wonder fill'd mine eye.

Her border was the purple tint
   Stole from the rising sun;
The whitest feather from the swan
   Upon her breast was dun:
Her placid smile of love and grace
   Must ev'ry bosom win;
The dew-drops glist'ning on her face,
   Show'd all was pure within.

But frost, on cold misfortune's wing,
   Hath crush'd her in the clay;
And ruthless fate hath rudely torn
   Each kindred branch away.

That wounded bark will never close
  But bleeding still remain !
How can ye blow, relentless winds,
  And nip my flower again!

———◆———

THE MOON WAS A-WAINING.

THE moon was a-waining,
  The tempest was over ;
Fair was the maiden,
  And fond was the lover.
But the snow was so deep,
  That his heart it grew weary ;
And he sunk down to sleep
  In the muirland so dreary.

Soft was the bed
  She had made for her lover
White were the sheets,
  And embroider'd the cover.
But his sheets are more white !
  And his canopy grander !
And sounder he sleeps
  Where the hill-foxes wander.

Alas ! pretty maiden !
  What sorrows attend you !

I see you sit shivering
  With lights at your window.
But long may you wait,
  Ere your arms shall enclose him ;
For still, still, he lies,
  With a wreath on his bosom.

How painful the task
  The sad tidings to tell you !
An orphan you were
  Ere this misery befell you.
And far in yon wild,
  Where the dead tapers hover,
So cold, cold, and wan,
  Lies the corpse of your lover !

———◆———

MARY AT HER LOVER'S GRAVE.

AIR—*Banks of the Dee.*

How swift flew the time when I stray'd with my
    Jamie.
  On flower-fringed valleys by Yarrow's fair
    stream !
But all I held precious is now taken from me !
  Sure every excess of delight is a dream !
Of fate I had never complained as unkindly
Had it to a bed or a prison confined me,

Reproach, shame, and ruin, before and behind me,
    Had Jamie been by me in every extreme.

But there, where my heart I had treasur'd for
            ever!
    Where all my affections on earth were bestow'd,
With one fatal stroke to destroy; and to sever
    Two bosoms with purest affection that glow'd!
Now dim is the eye that beam'd beauty and splen-
            dour!
And cold was the heart that was constant and ten
            der;
The sweet cherry lips to the worm must surrender,
    With wisdom, and truth, that delightfully flow'd.

Hence, comfort and pleasure! I cannot endure ye;
    Here, on this new grave, will I bid you adieu:
My reason is bleeding, and here will I bury
    That mirror, where clearly my misery I view.
O Thou! who the days of all mankind hast mea-
            sur'd!
A fate with my Jamie I'll cheerfully hazard!
Then drive me distracted to roam in the desart,
    Or bear me to him, that our joys may renew.

Else, even in death, my fond arms shall enclose
            him!
And my dust mix with his as we moulder away:
For here, with my hands, will I dig to his bosom,
    Where closely I'll cling, till the dawn of the day.

When the moon and the stars with a sob shall
    expire,
And the sun burst away like a flash of pale fire ;
Then, higher and higher, we'll jointly aspire
    To friendship that never shall end nor decay.

BONNY DUNDEE.

TUNE—*Comin' thro' the Rye.*

O WILL you gang down to the bush i' the meadow.
Your daddy an' mammy wi' me winna dread you ;
An' by the fair hand through the flowers I will
    lead you,
  An' sing you "the bonnets o' bonny Dundee?"
Wi' heart an' wi' hand, my dear lad, I'll gang wi'
    thee,
My daddy and mammy think nought to belie thee,
I ken ye'll do naething but kiss me an' lead me,
  An' sing me "the bonnets o' bonny Dundee.'

O, why fled thy angel, poor lovely Macmillen,
An' left thee to listen to counsel sae killin' ?
O, where were the feelin's o' that cruel villain,
  Who rifled that blossom. an' left it to die ?
How pale is that cheek that was rosy an' red ay !
To see that sunk e'e wad gar ony heart bleed ay !

O, wae to the wild-willow-bush i' the meadow.
O, dule to "the bonnets o' bonny Dundee!"

MY PEGGY AN' I.

TUNE—*Paddy Whack.*

I HAE a wee wifie, an' I am her man,
    My Peggy an' I, my Peggy an' I;
We waggle through life as weel as we can,
    An' wha's sae happy as Peggy an' I?
We hae a wee lassy will keep up our line.
    My Peggy an' I, my Peggy an' I,
I'm sure she is hers, an' I think she is mine,
    An' wha's sae happy as Peggy an' I?

We aftentimes dandle her upon the knee,
    My Peggy an' I, my Peggy an' I;
In ilka bit smile her dear mother I see,
    An' wha's sae happy as Peggy an' I?
O lang may she live to our honour an' joy,
    My Peggy an' I, my Peggy an' I,
An nae wicked fellow our darling decoy,
    For wha's sae happy as Peggy an' I?

Though Peggy an' I hae little o' gear,
    My Peggy an' I, my Peggy an' I;

We're healthy an' handy, an' never need fear,
  For wha's sae happy as Peggy an' I?
We sleep a' the night, an' we ply a' the day,
  My Peggy an' I, my Peggy an' I,
Baith vices an' follies lie out o' the way,
An' wha's sae happy as Peggy an' I?

Contented we are in the highest degree,
  My Peggy an' I, my Peggy an' I;
An' gratefu' to him wha contentment can gi'e,
  An' wha's sae happy as Peggy an' I?
Through life we will love, an' through life we
    will pray,
  My Peggy an' I, my Peggy an' I;
Then, sidie for sidie, we'll sleep i' the clay,
  An' wha's sae happy as Peggy an' I?

THE MINSTREL BOY.

The minstrel Boy to the glen is gone,
  In its deepest dells you'll find him,
Where echoes sing to his music's tone,
  And fairies listen behind him.
He sings of nature all in her prime,
  Of sweets that around him hover,
Of mountain heath and moorland thyme,
  And trifles that tell the lover.

11

How wildly sweet is the minstrel's lay,
  Through cliffs and wild woods ringing,
For, ah! there is love to beacon his way,
  And hope in the songs he's singing!
The bard may indite, and the minstrel sing,
  And maidens may chorus it rarely ;
But unless there be love in the heart within,
  The ditty may charm but sparely.

———◆———

THE GLOAMIN'.

AIR—*Mary weep nae mair for me.*

THE gloamin' frae the welkin high
  Had chas'd the bonny gowden gleam ;
The curtain'd east, in crimson dye,
  Hung heavy o'er the tinted stream :
The wild rose, blushing on the brier,
  Was set wi' draps o' shining dew,—
As big an' clear the bursting tear
  That row'd i' Betty's een sae blue.

She saw the dear, the little cot,
  Where fifteen years flew swiftly by,
An' mourn'd her shame, an' hapless lot,
  That forc'd her frae that hame to lie.
Though sweet an' mild the e'ening smil'd,
  Her heart was rent wi' anguish keen ;

The mavis ceas'd his music wild,
  An' wonder'd what her sobs could mean.

"It wasna kind to rob my mind
  Of a' its peace for evermair;
To blot my name wi' burning shame,
  An' mak my parents' hearts sae sair.
That hame how dare I enter now,
  Ilk honour'd face in tears to see,
Where oft I kneel'd, to hear the vow
  Was offer'd frae the heart for me!

"An' can I lo'e the treacherous man
  Wha wrought this dear an' deadly ill?
Wha blur'd wi' clouds my early dawn?
  Ah! waes my heart, I lo'e him still!
My heart abus'd! my love misus'd!
  My wretched fate wi' tears I see!
But maist, I fear, my parents dear,
  Gae mourning to the grave for me!"

LORD EGLINTON'S AULD MAN.

THE auld gudeman came hame at night,
  Sair wearied wi' the way;
His looks were like an evening bright,
  His hair was siller gray.

He spak' o' the days, lang past an' gane,
When life beat high in every vein;
When he was foremost on the plain
    On every blythsome day.

" Then blythly blush'd the mornin' dawn,
    An' gay the gloamin' fell;
For sweet content led ay the van,
    An' sooth'd the passions well;
Till wounded by a gilded dart,
When Jeanie's een subdued my heart,
I cherish'd ay the pleasing smart,—
    Mair sweet than I can tell.

" We had our griefs, we had our joys,
    In life's uneasy way;
We nourish'd virtuous girls an' boys,
    That now are far away:
An' she, my best, my dearest part,
The sharer o' each joy an' smart,
Each wish and weakness o' my heart,
    Lies moulderin' in the clay.

" The life o' man's a winter day:
    Look back, 'tis gone as soon:
But yet his pleasures halve the way
    An' fly before 'tis noon,
But conscious virtue still maintains
The honest heart through toils an' pains,

An' hope o' better days remains,
An' hauds the heart aboon.''

———•———

THE GUARDIAN ANGEL.

The dawning was mild, and the hamlet was wild,
 For it stood by an untrodded shore of the main,
When Duncan was rais'd from his slumber, amaz'd,
 By a voice at his door, that did shortly com-
  plain—
"Rise, Duncan, I perish!" his bosom was fir'd
 With feelings no language or pen can convey:
'Twas a voice he had heard, and with rapture ad-
  mir'd,
 Ere fatal Culloden had forc'd him away.

He flew to the rock that o'ershadow'd his cot,
 And wistfully look'd where his vision could
  reach;
He shouted—but only the echoes about
 Him answer'd, and billows that rush'd on the
  beach.
For the winds were at rest, but the ocean, opprest,
 Still heav'd like an earthquake, and broke on
  the shore;

The mist settled high on the mountains of Skye,
   And the wild howling storm ruffled nature no
      more.

He search'd every glen, every creek, every isle,
   Although every sense was with reason at strife;
When the sun blinked red o'er the hills of Argyll,
   He found his Matilda, his lady, his wife!
Resign'd to her fate, on a little green plat,
   Where a cliff intercepted the wanderer's way,
On her bosom so fair, and her fine yellow hair,
   The frost of the morning lay crisped and gray.

He wept like a child, while beside her he kneel'd,
   And cried, "O, kind Father, look down on my
      woe!
O, spare my sweet wife, and the whole of my life,
   My heart, for the gift, shall with gratitude
      glow!"
By care and attention she slowly recovers,
   And found herself lock'd in her husband's em-
      brace.
But, reader, if ever thou hast been a lover,
   Thy heart will outgo me, and furnish this space.

She said she had heard of his quiet retreat,
   And had come from the vale ere the tempest
      had low'r'd;

That the snow and the sleet had benumb'd her
  weak feet,
 And with hunger and cold she was quite over-
   power'd.
For her way she had lost, and the torrents she
  cross'd
 Had often nigh borne her away to the main;
But the night coming on, she had laid herself
  down,
 And prayed to her Maker, nor prayed she in
   vain.

" But did not you call at my cottage so early,
 When morning's gray streamers scarce crested
   the fell ?
A voice then did name me, and waken'd me fairly,
 And bade me arise, and the voice I knew well."
" Than where I was found, I was never more nigh
  thee :
 I sunk, overcome by toil, famine, and grief ;
Some pitying angel, then hovering by me,
 Has taken my voice to afford me relief."

Then down they both bow'd, and most solemnly
  vow'd
 To their great Benefactor his goodness to mind,
Both evening and morning unto them returning ;
 And well they perform'd the engagement we
  find

They both now are cold; but the tale they have
      told,
  To many, while gratitude's tears fell in store;
And whenever I pass by the bonny Glenasby,
  I mind the adventure on Morven's lone shore.

CAULD IS THE BLAST.

TUNE—*Lord Elcho's Delight.*

CAULD is the blast on the braes of Strahonan,
  The top of Ben-Wevis is driftin' wi' snaw!
The child i' my bosom is shiverin' an' moanin';
  Oh! pity a wretch that has naething ava.
My feet they are bare, and my cleathin is duddy,
  Yes, look gentle traveller; ance I was gay;
I hae twa little babies, baith healthy and ruddy
    But want will waste them and their mother
      away.

We late were as blythe as the bird on the Beauly,
  When the woodland is green, an' the flower on
      the lee:
But now he's ta'en frae us for ay, wha was truly
    A father to them, and a husband to me.
My Duncan supplied me, though far away lyin'
  Wi' heroes, the glory and pride of our isle;

But orders obeyin', and dangers defyin',
　He fell wi' Macleod on the banks of the Nile.

Pale, pale grew the traveller's visage so manly,
　An' down his grave cheek the big rollin' tear
　　ran;
I am not alone in the loss has befa'n me!*
　O wae to ambition the misery of man!
But go to my hall: to the poor an' the needy
　My table is furnish'd, an' open my door;
An' there I will cherish, an' there I will feed thee,
　And often together our loss we'll deplore."

———•———

THE SKYLARK.

BIRD of the wilderness,
　Blythesome and cumberless,
Sweet be thy matin o'er moorland and lea!
　Emblem of happiness,
　Blest is thy dwelling-place
O to abide in the desart with thee;
　Wild is thy lay and loud,
　Far in the downy cloud,
Love gives it energy, love gave it birth,
　Where on thy dewy wing

* The traveller was Macleod of Geanies, father to
the late brave Captain Macleod, who fell amongst his
countrymen in Egypt.

Where art thou journeying ?
Thy lay is in heaven, thy love is on earth.

O'er fell and fountain sheen,
O'er moor and mountain green,
O'er the red streamer that heralds the day,
Over the cloudlet dim.
Over the rainbow's rim,
Musical cherub, soar, singing, away ;
Then with the gloaming comes,
Low in the heather blooms,
Sweet will thy welcome and bed of love be ;
Emblem of happiness,
Blest is thy dwelling-place—
O to abide in the desart with thee !

CLASS SECOND.

Love Songs.

171

LOVE SONGS.

BONNY MARY.

WHERE Scaur rins whimpling 'mang the rocks,
   And wheels and boils in mony a linn,
A brisk young shepherd fed his flocks,
   Unus'd to guile, to strife, or din:
But love its silken net had thrown
   Around his breast so brisk and airy;
And his blue eyes wi' moisture shone,
   As thus he sung of Bonny Mary.

When o'er the Lowther's haughty head
   The morning breaks in streaks sae bonny
I climb the mountain's lonely side.
   For quiet rest I get na ony.
How sweet the brow on yon hill cheek!
   Where mony a weary hour I tarry;
For there I see the twisted reek
   Rise frae the cot where dwells my Mary.

Oft has the lark sung o'er my head,
    And shook the dew-draps frae her wing:
Oft hae my flocks forgot to feed,
    And round their shepherd form'd a ring
Their looks condole the lee-lang day,
    While mine are fix'd and canna vary:
Oft hae they listen'd to my lay
    Of faith and love to Bonny Mary.

When Phœbus mounts frae Crawford-muir,
    His gowden locks a' streaming gaily;
When morn has breath'd its fragrance pure,
    And life and joy rings through the valley;
I drive my flocks to yonder brook,
    The feeble in my arms I carry;
Then every lammie's harmless look
    Brings to my mind my Bonny Mary.

When gloamin' o'er the welkin steals,
    And haps the hills in sober gray;
And bitterns, in their airy wheels,
    Amuse the wanderer on his way;
Regardless of the wind and rain,
    With cautious step and prospect wary,
I often trace the lonely glen
    To get a sight of Bonny Mary.

When midnight draws her curtain deep,
    And lays the breeze amang the bushes,

And Scaur, wi' mony a winding sweep,
　　O'er rocks of reddle raves and rushes;
Though sunk in short and restless sleep,
　　My fancy wings her flight so airy
To where sweet guardian spirits keep
　　Their watch around the couch of Mary.

The exile may forget his home,
　　Where blooming youth to manhood grew;
The bee forget the honeycomb,
　　Nor with the spring his toil renew;
The sun may lose his light and heat;
　　The planets in their rounds miscarry;
But my fond heart shall cease to beat
　　When I forget my Bonny Mary.

MY BLYTHE AN' BONNY LASSIE.

Tune—*Neil Gow's Farewell to Whisky.*

How sair my heart nae man shall ken
When I took leave o' yonder glen,
Her faithful dames, her honest men,
　　Her streams sae pure an' glassy, O:
Her woods that skirt the verdant vale,
Her balmy breeze sae brisk an' hale,

Her flower of every flower the wale,
  My blythe an' bonny lassie, O !

The night was short, the day was lang,
An' ay we sat the birks amang,
Till o'er my head the blackbird sang
  Gae part wi' that dear lassie, O.
When on Lamgaro's top sae green
The rising sunbeam red was seen,
Wi' aching heart I left my Jean,
  My blythe an' bonny lassie, O.

Her form is gracefu' as the pine ;
Her smile the sunshine after rain ;
Her nature cheerfu', frank, an' kind,
  An' neither proud nor saucy, O.
The ripest cherry on the tree
Was ne'er sae pure or meek to see,
Nor half sae sweet its juice to me
  As a kiss o' my dear lassie, O.

Whate'er I do, where'er I be,
Yon glen shall ay be dear to me ;
Her banks an' howms sae fair to see ;
  Her braes sae green an' grassy, O :
For there my hopes are centred a' ;
An' there my heart was stown awa :
An' there my Jeanie first I saw,
  My blythe an' bonny lassie, O.

THE BRAES OF BUSHBY.

As glentin' cheerfu' simmer morn,
As I cam o'er the riggs o' Lorn,
I heard a lassie all forlorn
   Lamentin' for her Johnny, O.
Her wild notes pour'd the air alang;
The Highland rocks an' woodlands rang;
An' ay the o'erword o' her sang
   Was Bushby braes are bonny, O.

On Bushby braes where blossoms blow,
Where blooms the brier an' sulky sloe,
There first I met my only joe,
   My dear, my faithfu' Johnny, O.
The grove was dark, sae dark an' sweet!
Where first my lad an' I did meet;
The roses blush'd around our feet:
   Then Bushby braes were bonny, O.

Departed joys, how soft! how dear!
That frae my e'e still wrings the tear!
Yet still the hope my heart shall cheer
   Again to meet my Johnny, O.
The primrose saw, an' blue hare-bell,
But nane o' them our love can tell,
The thrilling joy I felt too well,
   When Bushby braes were bonny, O.

12

My lad is to the Baltic gane
To fight the proud an' doubtfu' Dane.
For our success my heart is fain ;
   But 'tis maistly for my Johnny, O.
Then, Cupid, smooth the German sea,
An' bear him back to Lorn an' me !
An' a' my life I'll sing wi' glee,
   The Bushby braes are bonny, O.

———◆———

BLYTHE AN' CHEERY.

Tune—*Blythe, blythe, an' merry was she.*

On Ettrick clear there grows a brier,
   An' mony a bonny bloomin' shaw ;
But Peggy's grown the fairest flower
   The braes o' Ettrick ever saw.
Her cheek is like the woodland rose ;
   Her e'e the violet set wi' dew ;
The lily's fair without compare,
   Yet in her bosom tines its hue.

Had I as muckle goud an' gear
   As I could lift unto my knee,
Nae ither lass but Peggy dear
   Should ever be a bride to me.

O she's blythe! an' O she's cheery!
  O she's bonny, frank, an' free!
The sternies bright, nae dewy night,
  Could ever beam like Peggy's e'e.

Had I her hame at my wee house,
  That stands aneath yon mountain high,
To help me wi' the kye an' ewes,
  An' in my arms at e'ening lie;
O sae blythe! an' O sae cheery
  O sae happy we wad be!
The lammie to the ewe is dear,
  But Peggy's dearer far to me.

But I may sigh an' stand abeigh,
  An' greet till I lose baith my een;
Though Peggy's smiles my heart beguiles,
  She disna mind my love a preen.
O I'm sad! O I'm sorry!
  Sad an' sorry may I be;
I may be sick, an' very sick,
  But I'll be desperate sweer to dee.

TO MISS JANE S——F.

Tune—*Arniston House.*

I WASNA sae soon to my bed yestreen;
  What ail'd me I never could close an e'e?
Was't Chalmers' sherry that thrill'd ilka vein?
  Or glamour yon gypsy has thrown upon me!
I'm certain twa een as bright I hae seen:
  An' every perfection in every degree!
Can naebody sing like Jeany yestreen,
  That sleep's sae completely departit frae me?

It isna her een, where modesty beams,
  Where sense an' good nature apparent we see
'Tis her sweet cherry lips, and her delicate form,
  Have left an impression where it shouldna be.
No, that's not the thing: 'tis an elegant ease
  Attending ilk action, though ever sae wee;
An' her sweet heavenly voice, sae to melody
    tun'd,
  It will ring in my lugs till the day that I dee.

It isna her een sae bonny an' blue,
  Nor nae single beauty astonishes me;
But the hale o' the lassie arises to view,
  As a model what womankind really may be.
Your love in a present I wadna receive,
  It wad mar sic a pure an' agreeable dream;

But only, if you think it prudent to give,
   A shepherd, dear Jeany, entreats your esteem.

THE BONNY LASS OF DELORAINE.

AIR—*Maid of Isla.*

STILL must my pipe lie idle by,
   And wordly cares my mind annoy?
Again its softest notes I'll try,
   So dear a theme can never cloy.
Last time my mountain harp I strung,
   'Twas she inspir'd the simple strain,
That lovely flower so sweet and young,
   The bonny lass of Deloraine.

How blest the breeze's balmy sighs
   Around her ruddy lips that blow;
The flower that in her bosom dies;
   Or grass that bends beneath her toe.
Her cheek's endued with powers, at will
   The rose's richest shade to drain;
Her eyes, what soft enchantments fill!
   The bonny lass of Deloraine.

Let Athol boast her birchen bowers,
   And Lomond of her isles so green;

And Windermere her woodland shores ;
   Our Ettrick boasts a sweeter scene :
For there the evening twilight swells
   With many a wild and melting strain ;
And there the pride of beauty dwells,
   The bonny lass of Deloraine.

If heaven shall keep her ay as good
   As now she's handsome, fair, and free,
The world may into Ettrick crowd,
   And Nature's first perfection see.
Glencoe has drawn the wanderer's eye,
   And Staffa in the western main !
These natural wonders ne'er can vie
   Wi' the bonny lass of Deloraine.

May health still cheer her beauteous face,
   And round her brows may honour twine ,
And Heaven preserve that breast in peace,
   Where meekness, love, and duty join.
But all her joys shall cheer my heart,
   And all her griefs shall give me pain ;
For never from my soul shall part
   The bonny lass of Deloraine.

I HAE LOST MY JEANY, O.

TUNE—*Lady Cunningham's Delight.*

O I HAE seen when fields were green,
  An' birds sae blythe an' cheery, O,
How swift the day wad pass away
  When I was wi' my deary, O:
But now I neither laugh nor sing,
  My looks are alter'd cleanly, O ;
I'll never like a lass again,
  Since I hae lost my Jeany, O;

Now I may grane an' greet my lane,
  An' never ane to heed me, O:
My claes, that ay were neat an' clean,
  Can scarce be said to cleed me, O:
My heart is sair, my elbows bare,
  My pouch without a guinea, O
I'll never taste o' pleasure mair,
  Since I have lost my Jeany, O.

O, Fortune ! thou hast us'd me ill
  Far waur than my deservin', O ;
Thrice o'er the crown thou'st knocked me down,
  An' left me haflins starvin', O :
Thy roughest blast has blawn the last
  My lass has used me meanly, O ;

Thy sharpest dart has pierc'd my heart,
  An' ta'en frae me my Jeany, O.

I'll nae mair strive, while I'm alive,
  For aught but missin' slavery, O;
This world's a stage, a pilgrimage,
  A mass o' lust an' knavery, O:
If fickle fame but save my name,
  An' frae oblivion screen me, O;
Then farewell fortune, farewell love,
  An' farewell bonny Jeany, O!

HERE, FIX'D BY CHOICE.

HERE, fix'd by choice, too long I staid
  Beside the lovely Flora;
Too fond to see the charming maid
  The cause of all my sorrow.
The rising sun each morning saw
  My passion fast augmenting,
Till she with Campbell cross'd the main,
  And left her love lamenting.

No curses on her head I'll crave;
  My blessing still attend her:
Whene'er I offer up my vows,
  My dear I'll ay remember.

Though mountains rise, and rivers roll,
   And oceans rage between us,
If death me spare, I'll search for her
   Through all the Carolinas.

Nor absence, time, nor balmy rest,
   Nor grief, nor tears, can ease me ;
I feel the time approaching fast
   When a clay-cold bed will please me.
Then rest my head upon yon hill,
   Where blows the blooming heather,
There first at Flora's feet I fell :
   There oft we sat together !

How happy would my charmer seem !
   How sorry when I left her !
I would not then have chang'd my seat
   With him that sway'd the sceptre.
My prospect glow'd with fairest flowers,
   From bliss no bounds to bar me :
Now dismal shades and dreary shores
   With rueful murmurs scare me.

There was a time, no more I'll see,
   I spent in mirth and ranging ;
There was time when I was gay,
   But times are always changing.
The times shall change, and moons shall wane,
    Yet I in love still languish ;

My tender heart must break in twain,
   Since nought can ease mine anguish.

I'M GANE A' WRANG, JAMIE.

Tune—*Up an' waur them a', Willie.*

" O what maks you sae dowie, lassie?
   What maks you sae cheerless?
For wit, an' fun, an harmless glee,
   My Peggy ay was peerless.
Ye're gane a' wrang, Peggy,
Ye're gane a' wrang, Peggy,
Ye've lost a frien', or catch'd the spleen,
   Or for some lad thought lang, Peggy."

" Yes, I hae catch'd a weary spleen
   Has banish'd a' my mirth, Jamie;
An' I hae lost the dearest frien'
   That e'er I ken'd on earth, Jamie.
I'm gane a' wrang, Jamie,
I'm gane a' wrang, Jamie,
For I've lien in an unco bed,
   Ayont an unco man, Jamie."

" Ah, waes my heart for what ye've done!
   Ye canna hide it lang, Peggy;

How could ye use your love sae ill ?
  Ye have done a' wrang, Peggy.
Ye've gane a' wrang, Peggy,
Ye've gane a' wrang, Peggy,
Ye promis'd aft to marry me,
  An' ay ere it was lang, Peggy.

" I'm unco wae to tak my leave ;
  But that's the thing maun be, Peggy
I'll never like a lass sae weel,
  Sin' I hae done wi' thee, Peggy.
Ye're gane a' wrang, Peggy,
Ye're gane a' wrang, Peggy,
Ye promis'd aft to marry me,
  An' ay ere it was lang, Peggy."

" I weel deserve my hapless lot,
  Ye war sae kind an' true, Jamie ;
My broken heart will ne'er forget
  How I've misused you, Jamie.
I'm gane a' wrang, Jamie,
I'm gane a' wrang, Jamie,
For I've lien in an unco bed,
  Ayont an unco man, Jamie.'

" My dear, I ken ye've done amiss ;
  But blame was far frae thee, Peggy :
I'll tell you what will gar you blush—
  The unco man was me Peggy.

We've done a' wrang, Peggy,
We've done a' wrang, Peggy;
We'll do the best that now remains,
    An' wed ere it be lang, Peggy.

* * *

THE HAY-MAKERS.

TUNE—*Coming through the Rye.*

" My lassie, how I'm charm'd wi' you
    'Tis needless now to tell;
Rut a' the flowers the meadow through,
    Ye're sweetest ay yoursel':
I canna sleep a wink by night,
    Nor think a thought by day;
Vour image smiles afore my sight
    Whate'er I do or say."

"Fye, Jamie! dinna act the part
    Ye'll ever blush to own;
Or try to wile my youthfu' heart
    Frae reason's sober throne:
Sic visions I can ne'er approve
    Nor ony wakin' dream;
Then trust sic fiery furious love
    I'd rather hae esteem."

" My bonny lassie, come away,
 I canna bide your frown ;
Wi' ilka flower, sae fresh an' gay,
 I'll deck your bosom round :
I'll pu' the gowan off the glen,
 The lily off the lee ;
The rose an' hawthorn bud I'll twine
 To make a bob for thee.''

" Aye, Jamie, ye wad steal my heart,
 An' a' my peace frae me ;
An' fix my feet within the net
 Ere I my error see.
I trow ye'll wale the flowery race
 My bosom to adorn ;
An' ye confess ye're gaun to place
 Within my breast a thorn.''

" How can my lassie be sae tart,
 An' vex me a' the day ?
Ye ken I lo'e wi' a' my heart,
 What wad ye hae me say ?
Ilk anxious wish an' little care
 I'll in thy breast confide,
An' a' your joys an' sorrows share,
 If ye'll become my bride.''

" Then tak my hand, ye hae my heart ;
 There's nane I like sae weel ;

An' Heaven grant I act my part
   To ane sae true an' leal.
This bonny day amang the hay,
   I'll mind till death us twine ;
An' often bless the happy day
   That made my laddie mine.''

THE BOGLES.

TUNE—*Logie o' Buchan.*

My bonny Eliza is fled frae the town,
An' left her poor Jamie her loss to bemoan ;
To mè 'tis a sad an' lamentable day ;
For the *bogles* have chas'd my Eliza away.
The Lowlands may weep, and the Highlands may
      smile,
In welcome to her that's the flower of our isle :
It's all for thy honour, ambitious Tay,
That the *bogles* have chas'd my Eliza away.

There's ae bitter thought has gi'en me muckle
      pain,
I fear I will never behold her again ;
I canna get quit o't, by night nor by day,
Since the *bogles* have chas'd my Eliza away.

O, sweet may the breeze be her mountains be-
          tween;
And sweet be her walks through her woodlands
          so green!
And sweet be the murmurs of fair winding Tay,
Since the *bogles* have chas'd my Eliza away!

I love her; I own it; I'll own it again;
If I had two friends on the earth, she was ane;
And now I can neither be cheerfu' nor gay,
Since the *bogles* have chas'd my Eliza away
May Heaven in kindness long shelter my flower.
So admir'd by the rich and belov'd by the poor!
Whose blessing will cheer her sweet bosom for
          aye,
Nor fairy, nor bogle, will chase it away.

BONNY JEAN.

Tune—*Prince William Henry's Delight.*

Sing on, sing on, my bonny bird,
   The sang ye sang yestreen, O,
When here, aneath the hawthorn wild,
   I met my bonny Jean, O.
My blude ran prinklin' through my veins,
   My hair began to steer, O;

My heart play'd deep against my breast!
    As I beheld my dear, O.

O weels me on my happy lot!
    O weels me on my dearie!
O weels me on the charmin' spot,
    Where a' combin'd to cheer me!
The mavis litit on the bush,
    The lavrock on the green, O;
The lily bloom'd, the daisy blush'd,
    But a' was nought to Jean, O.

Sing on, sing on, my bonny thrush,
    Be neither flee'd nor eerie;
I'll wad your love sits in the bush,
    That gars ye sing sae cheerie:
She may be kind, she may be sweet,
    She may be neat an' clean, O;
But O she's but a drysome mate,
    Compar'd wi' bonny Jean, O.

If love wad open a' her stores,
    An' a' her bloomin' treasures,
An' bid me rise, an' turn an' choice,
    An' taste her chiefest pleasures;
My choice wad be the rosy cheek,
    The modest beamin' eye, O;
The yellow hair, the bosom fair,
    The lips o' coral dye, O.

A bramble shade around her head,
　A burine poplin' by, O ;
Our bed the swaird, our sheet the plaid,
　Our canopy the sky, O.
An' here's the burn, an' there's the bush
　Around the flowrie green, O ;
An' this the plaid, an' sure the lass
　Wad be my bonny Jean, O.

Hear me, thou bonny modest moon !
　Ye sternies twinklin' high, O !
An' a' ye gentle powers aboon,
　That roam athwart the sky, O !
Ye see me gratefu' for the past,
　Ye saw me blest yestreen, O ;
An' ever till I breathe my last
　Ye'll see me true to Jean, O.

BONNY LEEZY.

Tune—O'er the Muir amang the Heather.

THOUGH I've enjoy'd my youth in health,
　An' liv'd a life both free an' easy !
Yet real delight I never felt
　Until I saw my bonny Leezy.
I've seen the Athol birk sae fair,
　The mountain pine, an' simple daisy ;

13

But nought I've seen can e'er compare
  Wi' the modest, gracefu' form o' Leezy.

I've seen tae hare trip o'er the dale,
  The lamb upon the lee sae gaily;
But when young Leezy trips the vale,
  For lively ease, she dings them fairly.
Her een, the dew-draps o' the morn!
  Hae gi'en my heart an unco heezy:
It canna be, that pride or scorn
  Can lodge within the breast o' Leezy.

I winna greet, I winna dee,
  Though love has made me something reezy;
But mirth shall ne'er gang down wi' me
  If aught befa' my bonny Leezy.
When her and I to rest are gane,
  May shepherds strew our graves wi' daisy!
And when o'er us they make their maen,
  Aye join my name wi' bonny Leezy!

NOW WELL MAY I.

TUNE—*Jacky Latin.*

Now well may I the haunts defy,
  Where love unlicens'd reign'd O;

Where since is pall'd an' conscience gall'd,
    And Nature's laws profan'd, O:
In yonder wood, above the flood,
    Conceal'd frae ilka eye, O,
Forby the bat, an' unbeaming wain,
    That slowly wheels on high, O.

Where blooms the brier, gie me my dear
    In innocence to woo, O;
An' ilka care on earth I'll leave
    This blessing to pursue, O.
Though troubles rise and wars increase,
    And discontents prevail, O,
We'll laugh and sing, and love our king,
    Till strength and vigour fail, O.

THE SHEEP SHEARING.

TUNE—*Bung your Eye i' the Morning.*

THE morning was fair, and the firmament sheen;
The valley was fresh, and the mountain was green;
When bonny young Jean, of our maidens the
        queen,
    Went o'er the dale to the shearing.
Her form was so fair, it was rather divine;
The rose-leaf and lily her features entwine

Her lip was the clover-flower moisten'd with
    wine ;
  Her manner was sweet and endearing.

Her voice was the music, so tuneful and true ;
Her hair was the sunbeam ; her eye was the dew,
The mirror where Love did his image review,
  And smile at the shadow so pleasing.
The knight, who was there at the shearing the
    ewes,
Says, "Farmer, your daughter's a beautiful rose:"
Then up to Miss Jeany he instantly goes,
  And kiss'd her, and aye would be teasing.

He led her and toy'd with her all the long day,
And gave her a ring set with jewels so gay :
"O ! meet me my dear," he would pressingly
    say,
  "This night in the bower by the river."
"I'll ask at my father," young Jeany replies ;
"I fain would be with you ; but if he denies"—
"Ah ! pray do not tell him," said he, with sur-
    prise,
  "And I'll love you, my Jeany, for ever."

"But what, my dear Sir, are you wanting with
    me ?
I'll never do aught but my father may see ;
He'll never refuse to intrust me with thee
  From evening till dawn of the morning."

She cries—"My dear father, the knight and your
     Jean
This night are to meet in the woodland so green,
To kiss and to prattle by mortal unseen,
  From evening till dawn of the morning."

The knight was abash'd and the farmer look'd
     sour.
"He mocks you, my jewel, go not to the bower."
"Then, sir, I am sorry 'tis out of my power
  To meet you this night by the river.
I'll always be proud of your gay company,
When my father permits I will wait upon thee."
Then, light as a lamb, she skipp'd over the lee,
  And left the poor knight in a fever,

"I ne'er saw a creature so lovely and sly;
Confound me, if ever I saw such an eye!
But every contrivance in life I will try
  To catch her alone by the river."
But all was in vain, she evaded him still,
Yet always receiv'd him with kindest good-will!
And now she's the lady of Merleton-hill,
  An' lovely an' loving as ever.

HOW FOOLISH ARE MANKIND.

TUNE—*The lone Vale.*

How foolish are mankind, to look for perfection
  In any poor changeling under the sun !
By nature, or habit, or want of reflection,
  To vices and folly we heedlessly run.
The man who is modest and kind in his nature,
  And open and cheerful in every degree :
Who feels for the woes of his own fellow-creature,
  Though subject to failings, is dear unto me.

Far dearer to me is the humble ewe-gowan,
  The sweet native violet, or bud of the broom,
Than fine foster'd flowers in the garden a-grow-
      ing,
  Though sweet be their savour, and bonny their
      bloom.
Far dearer to me is the thrush or the linnet,
  Than any fine bird from a far foreign tree ;
And dearer my lad, with his plaid and blue bonnet,
  Than all our rich nobles or lords that I see.

MY DEAR LITTLE JEANY.

Air—*Lack o' Gowd.*

" My dear little Jeany, what maks ye sae shy
An' saucy wi' Charley, whase horses an' kye
Gang wide on the meadow, his ewes on the lee ?
An' where will you see sic a laddie as he ?"
" Ah ! father, if you kend him as weel as I,
How ye wad despise him, his ewes an' his kye !
Whene'er we're our lane, on the meadow or hill,
Ilk word an' each action is tendin' to ill.

But Jamie's sae modest, that him I maun ruse ;
He'll beg for a kiss, which I canna refuse ;
He ne'er gies a look that a lassie needs fear,
Nor yet says a word but the warld may hear.
I ken, my dear father, ye like me sae weel,
That naething frae you I can ever conceal :
Young Charley is handsome, and gallant to see ;
But Jamie, though poorer, is dearer to me."

" My sweet little Jeany ! the pride o' my age !
Oh, how I'm delighted to hear you sae sage !
The forward, who makes the young maiden his
            prey
Is often carest, and the good sent away.
I like ye, my Jeany, as dear as my life ;
Ye've been a kind daughter, sae will ye a wife.

Then gree wi' your Jamie when he comes again;
From this time I'll count him a son o' my ain."

———◆———

WHEN THE KYE COMES HAME.

Come all ye jolly shepherds
  That whistle through the glen,
I'll tell ye of a secret,
  That courtiers dinna ken:
What is the greatest bliss
  That the tongue o' man can name?
'Tis to woo a bonny lassie
  When the kye comes hame.
    When the kye comes hame,
      When the kye comes hame,
    'Tween the gloaming and the mirk
      When the kye comes hame.

'Tis not beneath the coronet,
  Nor canopy of state,
'Tis not on couch of velvet,
  Nor arbour of the great—
'Tis beneath the spreading birk,
  In the glen without the name,
Wi' a bonny, bonny lassie,
  When the kye comes hame.

There the blackbird bigs his nest,
  For the mate he lo'es to see,
And on the topmost bough,
  O, a happy bird is he ;
Then he pours his melting ditty,
  And love is a' the theme,
And he'll woo his bonny lassie,
  When the kye comes hame.

When the blewart bears a pearl,
  And the daisy turns a pea,
And the bonnie lucken gowan
  Has fauldit up her ee,
Then the lavrock frae the blue lift,
  Draps down an' thinks nae shame
To woo his bonny lassie,
  When the kye comes hame.

See yonder pawky shepherd
  That lingers on the hill—
His yowes are in the fauld,
  And his lambs are lying still ;
Yet he downa gang to bed,
  For his heart is in a flame
To meet his bonny lassie,
  When the kye comes hame.

When the little wee bit heart
  Rises high in the breast,

And the little wee bit starn
   Rises red in the east,
O there's joy sae dear,
   That the heart can hardly frame
Wi' a bonny, bonny lassie,
   When the kye comes hame.

Then since all Nature joins
   In this love without alloy,
O, wha wad prove a traitor
   To Nature's dearest joy ?
Or wha wad choose a crown,
   Wi' its perils and its fame,
And miss his bonny lassie,
   When the kye comes hame.
     When the kye comes hame,
      When the kye comes hame,
      'Tween the gloaming and the mirk,'
     When the kye comes hame.

O, JEANIE, THERE'S NAETHING TO FEAR YE.

O, MY lassie, our joy to complete again,
   Meet me again i' the gloamin' my dearie;
Low down in the dell let us meet again—
   O! Jeanie, there's naething to fear ye!

Come, when the wee bat flits silent and eiry;
Come, when the pale face o' Nature looks weary,
    Love be thy sure defence,
    Beauty and innocence :—
O! Jeanie, there's naething to fear ye!

Sweetly blow the haw an' the rowan-tree,
  Wild roses speck our thicket so breery;
Still, still will our walk in the greenwood be
  O! Jeanie there's naething to fear ye :
List when the blackbird o' singing grows weary,
List when the beetle bee's bugle comes near ye!
    Then come with fairy haste,
    Light foot, an' beating breast :—
O! Jeanie, there's naething to fear ye!

Far, far will the bogle and brownie be;
  Beauty an' truth they darena come near it.
Kind love is the tie of our unity;
  A' maun love it, an' a' maun revere it.
Love makes the sang o' the woodland sae cheerie,
Love gars a' Nature look bonnie that's near ye;
    Love makes the rose sae sweet,
    Cowslip and violet!
O! Jeanie, there's naething to fear ye!

CLASS THIRD.

—

Humorous Songs.

—

HUMOROUS SONGS.

DOCTOR MONRO.

Tune—*Humours o' Glen.*

" Dear Doctor, be clever, and fling off your
        beaver ;
    Come bleed me, and blister me, do not be slow ;
I'm sick, I'm exhausted, my schemes they are
        blasted,
    And, all driven heels-o'er-head, Doctor Monro."
" Be patient, dear fellow, you foster your fever ;
    Pray what's the misfortune that bothers you
        so ?"
" O, Doctor ! I'm ruin'd ! I'm ruin'd for ever ;
    My lass has forsaken me, Doctor Monro.

" I meant to have married, and tasted the plea-
        sures,
    The sweets, the enjoyments, in wedlock that
        flow ;
But she's ta'en another, and broken my measures,
    And fairly confounded me, Doctor Monro."

207

" I'll bleed and I'll blister you, over and over;
  I'll master your malady ere that I go:
But raise up your head from below the bed cover,
  And give some attention to Doctor Monro.

" If Christy had wed you, she would have misled
          you,
  And laugh'd at your love with some handsome
          young beau.
Her conduct will prove it; but how could you love
          it ?"
    " I soon would have lam'd her, dear Doctor
        Monro."
" Each year brings a pretty young son, or a
        daughter;
  Perhaps you're the father; but how shall you
        know ?
You hugg them—her gallant is bursting with
        laughter"—
    " That thought's like to murder me, Doctor
        Monro."

" The boys cost you many a penny and shilling;
  You breed them with pleasure, with trouble,
        and woe :
But one turns a rake, and another a villain."—
    " My heart could not bear it, dear Doctor
        Monro."

"The lasses are comely, and dear to your bosom;
  But virtue and beauty has many a foe!
O think whát maý happen; just nipt in the blos-
      som!"—
  "Ah! merciful Heaven! cease, Doctor Monro.

"Dear Doctor, I'll thank you to hand me my
      breeches:
  I'm better; I'll drink with you ere that you go;
I'll never more sicken for women or riches,
  But love my relations and Doctor Monro.
I plainly perceive, were I wedded to Christy,
  My peace and my pleasure I must needs fore-
      go."
He still lives a bachelor; drinks when he's thirsty;
  And sings like a lark, and loves Doctor Monro.

LOVE'S LIKE A DIZZINESS.

Tune—*Paddy's Wedding.*

I LATELY liv'd in quiet ease,
  And never wish'd to marry, O;
But when I saw my Peggy's face,
  I felt a sad quandary, O.
Though wild as ony Athol deer,
  She has trepan'd me fairly, O;

14

Her cherry cheeks, an' een sae clear,
　　Harass me late an' early, O.
　　　　O! love! love! laddie.
　　　　　　Love's like a dizziness!
　　　　　It winna let a puir body
　　　　　　Gang about his business.

To tell my feats this single week
　　Wad mak a curious diary, O:
I drave my cart against a dyke,
　　My horses in a miry, O:
I wear my stockings white and blue,
　　My love's sae fierce an' fiery, O:
I drill the land that I should plough,
　　An' plough the drills entirely, O.—O! love! &c.

Soon as the dawn had brought the day,
　　I went to theek the stable, O;
I coost my coat, and ply'd away
　　As fast as I was able, O.
I wrought a' morning out an' out
　　As I'd been redding fire, O;
When I had done, and look'd about,
　　Gude faith it was the byre, O!—O! love! &c.

Her wily glance I'll ne'er forget;
　　The dear, the lovely blinkin' o't,
Has pierc'd me through an' through the heart,
　　An' plagues me wi' the prinklin' o't.

I try'd to sing, I try'd to pray,
   I try'd to drown't wi' drinkin, o't;
I try'd wi' toil to drive't away,
   But ne'er can sleep for thinkin' o't.—O! love!

Were Peggy's love to hire the job,
   An' save my heart frae breakin', O,
I'd put a girdle round the globe,
   Or dive in Corryvrekin, O;
Or howk a grave at midnight dark
   In yonder vault sae eerie, O;
Or gang an' spier for Mungo Park
   Through Africa sae dreary, O.—O! love! &c.

Ye little ken what pains I prove!
   Or how severe my plisky, O!
I swear I'm sairer drunk wi' love
   Than e'er I was wi' whisky, O;
For love has rak'd me fore an' aft,
   I scarce can lift a leggy, O:
I first grew dizzy, then gaed daft,
   An' now I'll dee for Peggy, O.—O! love! &c.

AULD ETTRICK JOHN.

Tune—*Rothiemurchus' Rant.*

THERE dwalt a man on Ettrick side,
　　An honest man I wot was he ;
His name was John, and he was born
　　A year afore the thirty-three.
He had a wife when he was young,
　　But she had deit, an' John was wae ;
He wantit land, at length did gang
　　To court the lassie o' the brae.

Auld John came daddin' down the hill,
　　His arms was waggin, manfullie ;
He thought his shadow look'd na ill,
　　As aft he keek'd aside to see.
His shoon were four pound weight a-piece,
　　On ilka leg a ho had he ;
His doublet strang was large an' lang,
　　His breeks they hardly reach'd his knee.

His coat was threed-about wi' green,
　　The mouds* had wrought it muckle harm ;
The pouches war an ell atween,
　　The cuf was faldit up the arm.

* Moths.

He wore a bonnet on his head,
  The bung upon his shoulders lay,
An' by the neb ye wad hae red
  That Johnnie view'd the milky-way.

But yet for a' his antic dress,
  His cheeks wi' healthy red did glow;
His joints war knit, an' firm like brass,
  Though siller gray his head did grow:
An' John, although he had nae lands,
  Had twa gude kye amang the knowes;
A hunder pund i' honest hands,
  An' sax-an'-thretty doddit yowes.

An' Nelly was a bonny lass,
  Fu' sweet an' ruddy was her mou';
Her een war like twa beads o' glass,
  Her brow was white like Cheviot woo;
Her cheeks were bright as heather-bells,
  Her bosom like December snaw,
Her teeth as pure as eggs' shells,
  Her hair was like the hoddy craw.

"Gudewife," quo' John, as he sat down,
  "I'm come to court your daughter Nell;
An' if I die immediately,
  She sall hae a' the gear hersel.
An' if I chance to hae a son,
  I'll breed him up a braw divine;

An' if ilk wish turn out a wean,
    There's little fear that we hae nine."

Now Nelly thought, an' aye she leugh,
    " Our lads are a' for sogers gane ;
Young Tam will kiss an' toy enengh,
    But he o' marriage talketh nane.
When I am laid in Johnnie's bed,
    Like hares or lav'rocks I'll be free ;
I'll busk me braw an' conquer a'—
    Auld Johnnie's just the man for me."

Wi' little say he wan the day,
    She soon became his bonny bride ;
But ilka joy is fled away
    Frae Johnnie's canty ingle side.
She frets an' greets, an' visits aft,
    In hopes some lad will see her hame ;
But never ane will be sae daft
    As tent auld Johnnie's flisky dame.

An' John will be a gaishen soon ;
    His teeth are frae their sockets flown ;
The hair peel'd aff his head aboon ;
    His face is milk-an'-water grown :
His legs, that firm like pillars stood,
    Are now grown toom an' unco sma' ;
She's reav'd him sair o' flesh an' blood,
    An' peace o' mind—the warst ava.

Let ilka lassie tak a man,
 An' ilka callan tak a wife;
But youth wi' youth gae hand in hand,
 Or tine the sweetest joys o' life,
Ye men wha's heads are turnin' gray,
 Wha to the grave are hastin' on,
Let reason aye your passion sway,
 An' mind the fate o' Ettrick John.

An' a' ye lasses plump and fair,
 Let pure affection guide your hand,
Nor stoop to lead a life o' care,
 Wi' wither'd age, for gear or land.
When ilka lad your beauty slights,
 An' ilka smile shall yield to wae,
Ye'll mind the lang an' lanesome nights
 O' Nell, the lassie o' the brae.

BONNY BEETY.

TUNE—*Tow row row.*

" I was a weaver, young an' free,
 Sae frank an' cheery aye to meet wi',
Until wi' ane unwary e'e
 I view'd the charms o' Bonny Beety.

Lack a day !
Far away
Will I gae,
If I lose her.

"I tauld her I had got a wound
  Through sark an' waistcoat frae her sweet e'e ;
She said it ne'er should do't again,
  An' off like lightning flew my Beety.
      Luckless day !
      May I say,
      When my way
      Led to Beety.

"Ae day she cam wi' hanks o' yarn,
  When wi' my wark my face was sweety ;
She said I was a chrieshy thief,
  An' ne'er should get a kiss o' Beety.
      O ho, ho, hon !
      Now I'm gone,
      Love has pro'en
      A weaver's ruin.

"She laughs at me an' at my loom,
  An' wi' the herd has made a treaty ;
But wae light on this clouted shoon,
  How durst he e'er attempt my Beety ?
      O how blind,
      Eyes an' mind,

Womankind
Are to their profit!

"But by my shuttle now I swear,
  An' by the beam, if Wattie meet me,
I'll cut his throat frae ear to ear—
  I'll lose my life or gain my Beety,
        Blood an' guts!
        Jades an' sluts!
        I'll lose my wits,
        If I lose Beety."

Thus sang the weaver at his wark,
  An' wi' pure grief was like to greet aye,
When Charlie brought a letter ben,
  He thought he ken'd his Beety.
        Happy day,
        Did he say,
        When my way
        Led to Beety.

He read—"Dear sir, my wedding-day
  Is Friday neist, an' you maun meet me,
To wish me joy, an' drink my health,
  An' dine wi' me—your servant Beety."
        "O ho, hon
        Now I'm gone,
        Love has pro'en
        A weaver's ruin.

He raise—sat down—an' raise again—
  Ask'd Charlie if the day was sleety;
Then through his head he popp'd the lead,
  An' died a fool for love o' Beety.
        The web is red,
        Beety's wed,
        Will is dead,
        An' all is over.

AYONT THE MOW AMANG THE HAY.

TUNE—*Andrew wi' his cutty Gun.*

BLYTHLY hae I screw'd my pipes,
  An' blythly play'd the lee-lang day,
An' blyther been wi' bonny Bess
  Ayont the mow amang the hay.
When first I saw the bonny face
  O Bessie, bloomin' in her teens,
She wyl'd away this heart o' mine,
  An' ca'd it fou o' corkin' preens.

" At e'en when a' the lave gae lie,
  An' grannie steeks her waukrife e'e,
Steal out when I the winnock tap,
  Ahint the ha' I'll meet wi' thee."

She leugh an' bad me let her hame,
   Her mither sair wad flyte an' scauld ;
But ere I quat my bonny Bess
   Anither tale I trow she tauld.

On Tysday night, fou weel I wat,
   Wi' hinny words I row'd my tongue,
Raught down my plaid, an stievely stak
   Untill my neive a hazel rung.
Now whan I con'd my artless tale
   Gaun linkin' owre the lilie lea,
Fou weel I trow'd that ilka bush
   Some jeering question speir'd at me.

The bleeter cry'd frae yont the loch,
   " O hoolie, hoolie—whare ye gaun ?"
The craik reply'd frae 'mang the corn,
   " Turn out your taes, my bonny man."
An' soon I faund wi' shiv'rin' shanks,
   My heart play dunt through basfou fear,
Whan glow'rin' owre the kail-yard dyke
   To see gin a' the coast was clear ;

An' there, like ony nightly thief,
   Wi' eerie swither lour'd awhile,
Till rallying ilka traitor nerve,
   I lightly laup outowr the stile ;
Syne gae the glass twa cannie pats,
   An' Bessie bade na lang frae me ;

The rousty lock was ullied weel,
An' ilka hinge o' cheepin' free.

O say, ye haly Minstrel band,
Wha saw the saft, the silken hour,
Though joys celestial on ye wait,
Say, was your bliss mair chastely pure?
Blythly hae I screw'd my pipes,
An' blythly play'd the lee-lang day,
An, happy been wi' bonny Bess
Ayont the mow amang the hay,

THE DRINKIN', O.

A SANG FOR THE LADIES.

TUNE—*Dunbarton Drums.*

O WAE to the wearifu' drinkin', O!
That foe to reflection and thinkin', O!
        Our charms are gi'en in vain!
        Social conversation's gane!
For the rattlin' o' guns an' the drinkin', O.

O why will you ply at the drinkin', O?
Which to weakness will soon lead you linkin', O;
        These eyes that shine sae bright
        Soon will be a weary sight,
When ye're a' sittin' noddin' an' winkin', O!

For ever may we grieve for the drinkin', O!
The respect that is due daily sinkin', O!
    Our presence sair abused,
    An' our company refused,
An' its a' for the wearifu' drinkin', O!

O drive us not away wi' your drinkin', O!
We like your presence mair than ye're think-
      in', O!
    We'll gie ye anither sang,
    An' ye're no to think it lang,
For the sake o' your wearifu' drinkin', O!

Sweet delicacy, turn us to blinkin', O!
For by day the guns and swords still are clink-
      in', O!
    An' at night the flowin' bowl
    Bothers ilka manly soul,
Then there's naething but beblin' an' drinkin', O!

Gentle Peace, come an' wean them frae drink-
      in', O!
Bring the little footy boy wi' you winkin', O!
    Gar him thraw at ilka man,
    An' wound as deep he can,
Or we're ruin'd by the wearifu' drinkin, O!

GRACIE MILLER.

Tune—Braes of Balquhidder.

"Little, queer bit auld body,
  Whar ye gaun sae late at e'en?
Sic a massy auld body
  I saw never wi' my een."
"I'm gaun to court the bonniest lass
  That ever stepp'd in leather shoe."
"But little shabby auld body,
  Where's the lass will look at you?

"Ere I war kiss'd wi' ane like you,
  Or sic a man cam to my bed,
I'd rather kiss the hawkit cow,
  An' in my bosom tak a taed.
Wha ever weds wi' sic a stock
  Will be a gibe to a' the lave:
Little, stupit auld body,
  Rather think upon your grave."

"But I'm sae deep in love wi' ane,
  I'll wed or die, it maks na whether:
O! she's the prettiest, sweetest queen,
  That ever brush'd the dew frae heather;
The fairest Venus ever drawn
  Is naething but a bogle till her;

She's fresher than the morning dawn,
An' hark—her name is Gracie Miller."

She rais'd her hands; her een they reel'd;
Then wi' a skirt outowr she fell;
An' aye she leugh, an' aye she squeel'd,
"Hey! mercy! body, that's mysel'!"
Then down he hurkled by her side,
An' kiss'd her hand, an' warmly woo'd her:
An' whiles she leugh, an' whiles she sigh'd,
An' lean'd her head upon his shoulder.

"O pity me, my bonny Grace!
My words are true, ye needna doubt 'em,
Nae man can see your bonny face
An' keep his senses a' about him."
"Troth, honest man, I kend lang syne
Nae ither lass could equal wi' me;
But yet the brag sae justly mine
Was tint, till you hae chanc'd to see me.

Though ye want yudith, gear, an' mense,
Ye hae a dash o' amorous fire;
Ye hae good taste, an' sterling sense,
An ye sal hae your heart's desire."
O, woman! woman! after death,
If that vain nature still is given,
An' diels get leave to use their breath,
They'll flatter ye into hell frae heaven.

BIRNIEBOUZLE.

TUNE—*Braes of Tullymet.*

"WILL ye gang wi' me, lassie,
  To the braes o' Birniebouzle?
Baith the earth an' sea, lassie,
  Will Prob to fend ye.
I'll hunt the otter an' the brock;
The hart, the hare, an' heather-cock;
An' pu' the limpat off the rock,
  To fatten an' to fend ye.

"If ye'll gae wi' me, lassie,
  To the braes o' Birniebouzle,
Till the day we dee, lassie,
  Ye sall aye hae plenty:
The peats I'll carry in a skull;
The cod an' ling wi' lines I'll pull;
An' reave the eggs o' mony a gull,
  To mak ye dishes dainty.

"Sae cheery will ye be, lassie,
  I' the braes o' Birniebouzle;
Donald Gun and me, lassie,
  Ever will attend ye.
Though we hae nouther milk nor meal,
Nor lamb nor mutton, beef nor veal
We'll fank the porpy an' the seal,
  An' that's the way to fend ye.

" An' ye sal gang sae braw, lassie,
   At the kirk o' Birniebouzle ;
Wi' littit brogs an' a' lassie,
   Wow but ye'll be vaunty :
An' ye sal wear, when you are wed,
The kirtle an' the Highland plaid,
An' sleep upon a heather bed,
   Sae cozy an' sae canty."

" If ye will marry me, laddie,
   At the kirk o' Birniebouzle ;
My chiefest aim shall be, laddie,
   Ever to content ye :
I'll bait the line an' bear the pail,
An' row the boat an' spread the sail,
An' dadd the clotters wi' a flail,
   To mak our tatoes plenty."

" Then come awa wi' me, lassie,
   To the braes o' Birniebouzle ;
An' since ye are sae free, lassie,
   Ye sal ne'er repent ye ;
For ye sal hae baith tups an' ewes,
An' gaits an' swine, an' stots an' cows,
An' be the lady o' my house,
   An, that may weel content ye."

15

LIFE IS A WEARY COBBLE O' CARE.

TUNE—*Bob o' Dumblane.*

LIFE is a weary, weary, weary.
Life is a weary cobble o' care ;
    The poets mislead you,
    Wha ca' it a meadow,
For life is a puddle o' perfect despair.
We love an' we marry, we fight an' we vary,
Get children to plague an' confound us for aye !
    Our daughters grow limmers,
    Our sons they grow sinners,
An' scorn ilka word that a parent can say.

Man is a steerer, steerer, steerer,
Man is a steerer, life is a pool ;
    We wrestle an' fustle,
    For riches we bustle,
Then drap in the grave, an' leave a' to a fool.
    Youth again could I see,
    Women should wilie be,
Ere I were wheedled to sorrow an pain ;
    I should take care o' them,
    Never to marry them ;
Hang me if buckled in wedlock again.

JACK AND HIS MOTHER,

TUNE—*Jackson's Cog in the Morning.*

" Now, mother, since a' our young lasses ye saw,
Yestreen at the wedding, sae trig an' sae braw,
Say, wasna my Peggy the flower o' them a'
 Our table an' party adorning ?
Her form is so fair, an' her features so fine ;
Her cheek like the lily anointit wi' wine ;
The beam o' her bonny blue e'e does outshine
 The stern that appears in the morning."

" Awa, ye poor booby ! your skill is but sma' !
If ye marry Peggy ye'll ruin us a' :
She lives like a lady, an' dresses as braw :
 But how will she rise i' the morning ?
She'll lie in her bed till eleven, while ye
Maun rise an' prepare her her toast an' her tea :
Her friends will be angry, an' send ye to sea,
 Dear Jocky, be wise an' tak warning."

" O mother ! sic beauty I canna forego !
I've sworn I will have her, come weal or come
   woe ;
An' that wad be perjury, black as a crow,
 To leave her an' think of another."
" An' if ye do wed her, your prospects are fine ;
In meal-pocks an' rags ye will instantly shine :

Gae break your mad vow, an' the sin shall be mine;
  O pity yoursel' an' your mother ?"

"I'm sure my young Peggy is handsome an' gay:
I spoke to her father this very same day,
An' tauld him I was for his daughter away."
  " Dear Jocky! what said he this morning ?"
"He said he wad gie me a horse an' a cow,
A hunder gude ewes, an' a pack o' his woo,
To stock a bit farm at the back o' the brow,
  An' gie Maggy wark i' the morning."

"Troth Peggy is bonny, and handsome I trow ;
An' really 'tis dangerous breaking a vow :
Then tak her ; my blessing on Peggy an' you
  Shall tarry baith e'ening and morning."
So Jocky an' Peggy in wedlock were bound ;
The bridal was merry, the music did sound ;
They went to their bed, while the glass it gaed
      round,
  An' a' wish'd them joy, i' the morning.

ATHOL CUMMERS.

DUNCAN lad, blaw the bummers!
    Play me round the Athol Cummers!
A' the din o' a' the drummers
    Canna rouse like Athol Cummers.
When I'm dowie, weet, or weary,
Soon my heart grow light an' cheery,
When I hear the sprightly num'ers
Of my dear, my Athol Cummers.
                    Duncan lad, &c.

When the fickle lasses vex me;
When the cares of life perplex me;
When I'm fley'd wi' frightfu' rumours,
Then I cry for Athol Cummers.
                    Duncan lad, &c.

'Tis a cure for a' disasters;
Kebbit ewes, an crabbit masters;
Drifty nights, an' dripping summers,
A' my joy is Athol Cummers.
                    Duncan lad, &c.

Athol banks and braes are bonny,
Fairer nane in Caledony;
But a' her woods, an' sweetest summers,
Canna please like Athol Cummers.

                              Duncan lad, &c.

WILLIE WASTLE.

TUNE—*Macfarlane's Reel.*

WILLIE WASTLE lo'ed a lass
  Was bright as ony rainbow!
A pretty dear I wat she was,
  But saucy an' disdainfu';
She cortit was by many a lad,
  Wha teas'd her late an' early;
An' a' the wiles that Willie had
  Could scarcely gain a parley.

The western sea had drown'd the sun;
  The sternies blinkit clearly;
The moon was glentin' o'er the glen;
  To light him to his deary.
She dwalt amang the mountains wild,
  Nae wood nor bower to shade her;
But O! the scene look'd sweet an' mild,
  For luve o' them that staid there.

The cock that craw'd wi' yelpin' voice,
  Nae claronet sae grand, O;
The bonny burnie's purlin' noise
  Was sweet as the piano.
The little doggy at the door,
  Into his arms he caught it,

An' hugg'd an' sleek'd it o'er an' o'er,
　For luve o' them that aught it,

The house was thráng, the night was lang,
　The auld gudewife bethought her,
To tak a lair was naething wrang
　Beside her bonny doughter.
Sly Willie enter'd unperceiv'd
　To wake his charming Annie,
An' straight his jealous mind believ'd
　The wife was shepherd Sawny.

Though milder than the southern breeze,
　When July's odours waftin',
Yet now his passion made a heeze,
　An' a' his reason left him;
He gae the kerlin sic a swinge,
　He didna stand on prattlin',
Till down her throat, like birstled beans,
　He gart her teeth gang rattlin'.

The doggy fawn'd, but gat a drub
　Frae Willie's hand uncivil;
The burn was grown a drumly dub;
　The cock a scirlin' devil.
The place appear'd a wilderness,
　A desart, dank an' dreary;
For O! alas! the bonny lass
　Nae mair could mak it cheery!

O love ! thou ray of life divine !
　If rosy virtue guide thee,
What sense or feeling half sae fine .
　What blessings too abide thee !
But jealousy, thy neighbour sour,
　Deforms the finest feature,
An' maks a gloomy shade to lour
　O'er fairest scenes in nature.

WHEN MAGGY GANGS AWAY.

O WHAT will a' the lads do
　When Maggy gangs away ?
O what will a' the lads do
　When Maggy gangs away ?
There's nae heart in a' the glen
　That disna dread the day.
O what will a' the lads do
　When Maggy gangs away ?

Young Jock has taen the hill for't—
　A waefu' wight is he ;
Poor Harry's taen the bed for't,
　An' laid him down to dee ;
An' Sandy's gane unto the kirk,
　And learnin' fast to pray.
And, O, what will the lads do
　When Maggy gangs away ?

The young laird o' the Lang-Shaw
  Has drunk her health in wine ;
The priest has said—in confidence—
  The lassie was divine—
And that is mair in maiden's praise
  Than ony priest should say :
But, O, what will the lads do
  When Maggy gangs away ?

The wailing in our green glen
  That day will quaver high,
'Twill draw the redbreast frae the wood,
  The laverock from the sky ;
The fairies frae their beds o' dew
  Will rise an' join the lay
An' hey ! what a day will be
  When Maggy gangs away !

AULD JOHN BORTHICK.

Tune—*The Toper's Delight.*

Auld John Borthick is gane to a weddin',
  Frae Edinburgh owr to the east neuk o' Fife ;
His cheeks they war thin, an' his colour was fadin',
  But auld John Borthick was mad for a wife.
His heart was as light as the lammie's in July,
  An' saft as the mushroom that grows on the lee ;

For bonny Miss Jeany had squeez'd it to ulzie
  Wi' ae wily blink o' her bonny blue e'e.

He sat in a neuk in confusion an' anguish;
  His gravat was suddled, but that wasna a';
His head wasna beld, but his brow was turn'd
          langish;
  His teeth warna out, but they war turnin' sma';
He saw bonny Jeany afore him was landit;
  He saw bonny Jeany was favour'd by a';
By lairds an' by nobles respectfully handit;
  An' wow but Miss Jeany was bonny an' braw!

"Alas!" quo' John Borthick, "they'll spoil the
          poor lassie,
  An' gar her believe that she carries the bell;
I'll ne'er hae a wife sae upliftit an' saucy;
  I cou'dna preserve her a month to mysel'.
But yet she's sae handsome, sae modest, an' rosy,
  The man wha attains her is blest for his life;
My heart is a' earning to lie in her bosy.
    Oh! dear!" quo' John Borthick, "gin I had a
          wife!"

Lang Geordie was tipsy; he roar'd an' he rantit;
  He danc'd an' he sang, an' was brimfu' o' glee;
Of riches, of strength, an' of favour he vauntit:
  No man in the world sae mighty as he.
But in cam his wife; he grew sober an' sulky;
  She bade him gang hame as he valued his life;

Then cuff'd him, an' ca'd him an ass an' a monkey,
    "Ha! faith!" quo' John Borthick, "I'll ne'er
        hae a wife."

The bride an' bridegroom to their bed they retir'd;
    Miss Jeany was there, an' John Borthick an' a':
He look'd at Miss Jeany, his heart was inspired;
    Some said that the tears frae his haffits did fa'.
He saw the bridegroom tak the bride in his bosom;
    He kiss'd her, caress'd her, an' ca'd her his life;
John turn'd him about; for he couldna compose
        him:
    "O, Lord!" quo' John Borthick, "gin I had
        a wife!"

The mornin' appear'd, an the cobble was ready;
    John Borthick was first at the end of the bay:
But oh! to his sorrow he miss'd the sweet lady;
    A beau had her under his mantle away.
In less than a fortnight John Borthick was mar-
        ried
    To ane wha might weel be the joy o' his life:
But yet, wi' confusion an' jealousy worried,
    He curses the day that he married a wife.

CLASS FOURTH.

National Songs.

NATIONAL SONGS.

BAULDY FRASER.

Tune—*Whigs o' Fife.*

My name is Bauldy Fraser, man,
I'm puir an' auld, an' pale an' wan,
I brak my shin, an' tint a han'
    Upon Culloden lee, man.
Our Highlan' clans war bauld an' stout,
An' thought to turn their faes about,
But gat that day a desperate rout,
    An' owre the hills did flee, man.

Sic hurly-burly ne'er was seen,
Wi' cuffs, an' buffs, an' blindit een,
While Highlan' swords o' metal keen,
    War gleamin' grand to see, man.
The cannons rowtit in our face,
An' brak our banes an' raive our claes;
'Twas then we saw our ticklish case
    Atween the deil an' sea, man.

239

Sure Charlie an' the brave Lochyell
Had been that time beside theirsell,
To plant us in the open fell
     In the artillery's e'e, man :
For had we met wi' Cumberland
By Athol braes or yonder strand,
The bluid o' a' the savage band
     Had dy'd the German sea, man.

But down we drappit dadd for dadd ;
I thought it sude hae put me mad,
To see sae mony a Highlan' lad
     Lie bluthrin' on the brae, man.
I thought we ance had won the fray ;
We smasht ae wing till it gae way ;
But the other side had lost the day,
     An' skelpit fast awa, man.

When Charley wi' Macpherson met,
Like Hay, he thought him back to get ;
" We'll turn," quo' he, " an' try them yet ;
     We'll conquer or we'll dee, man."
But Donald jumpit owre the burn,
An' sware an aith she wadna turn,
Or sure she wad hae cause to mourn ;
     Then fast away did flee, man.

O ! had you seen that hunt o' death .
We ran until we tint our breath,

Aye looking back for fear o' skaithe
    Wi' hopeless shinin' e'e, man.
But Britain ever may deplore
That day upon Drumossie moor,
Whar thousands ta'en war drench'd in gore,
    Or hang'd outowr a tree, man.

O! Cumberland! what mean'd ye then
To ravage ilka Highlan' glen?
Our crime was truth an' love to ane;
    We had nae spite at thee, man.
An' you or yours may yet be glad
To trust the honest Highlan' lad;
The bonnet blue an' belted plaid
    Will stand the last o' three, man.

SCOTIA'S GLENS.

Tune—*Lord Ballandine's Delight.*

'Mong Scotia's glens and mountains blue,
Where Gallia's lilies never grew,
Where Roman eagles never flew
    Nor Danish lions rallied:
Where skulks the roe in anxious fear,
Where roves the stately, nimble deer,
There live the lads to freedom dear,
    By foreign yoke ne'er galled.

16

There woods grow wild on every hill;
There freemen wander at their will;
Sure Scotland will be Scotland still
    While hearts so brave defend her.
"Fear not, our Sov'reign liege," they cry,
"We've flourish'd fair beneath thine eye;
For thee we'll fight, for thee we'll die,
    Nor aught but life surrender.

"Since thou hast watch'd our every need,
An' taught our navies wide to spread,
The smallest hair from thy gray head
    No foreign foe shall sever.
Thy honour'd age in peace to save
The sternest host we'll dauntless brave,
Or stem the fiercest Indian wave,
    Nor heart nor hand shall waver.

"Though nations join yon tyrant's arm,
While Scotia's noble blood runs warm,
Our good old man we'll guard from harm,
    Or fall in heaps around him.
Although the Irish harp were won,
And England's roses all o'errun,
'Mong Scotia's glens, with sword and gun,
    We'll form a bulwark round him."

THE JUBILEE.

Air—*Miss Carmichael's Minuet.*

Who will not join the lay,
And hail the auspicious day
That first gave great George the sway
    Over our Island?
Fifty long years are gone
Since he first filled the throne ;
And high honours has he won
    On sea and by land.

Think on his heart of steel ;
Think on his life so leal ;
Think how he's watch'd our weal,
    Till seiz'd with blindness !
In mercy first sent to us ;
In love so long lent to us :
Grateful let's vent our vows
    For Heaven's kindness.

No foeman dare steer to us,
Nor tyrant come near to us,
Of all that's dear to us
    He's the defender.
Raise the song ! raise it loud !
Of our old king we're proud !

George the just ! George the good !
  Still reigns in splendour !

THE AULD HIGHLANDMAN.

Tune—Killiecrankie.

HERSEL pe aughty eirs an' twa,
  Te twanty-tird o' May, man;
She twall amang te Heelan hills,
  Apoon te reefer Spey, man.
Tat eir tey faucht te Shirramoor,
She first peheld te licht, man;
Tey shot my fater in tat stour—
  A plaguit, vexan spite, man.

I've feucht in Scotlan' here at hame,
  In France an' Shermanie, man;
An' cot tree tespurt pluddy oons
  Peyon te 'Lantic sea, man.
Put wae licht on te nasty gun,
  Tat ever she pe porn, man;
File coot claymore te tristle guard
  Her leaves pe nefer torn, man.

Ae tay I shot, an' shot, an' shot,
  Fan eer it kam my turn, man;

Put a' te foirs tat I cood gie,
   My powter wadna purn, man.
A filthy loun kam wi' his gun,
   Resolvt to too me harm, man;
An' wi' te dirk upon her nose
   Ke me a pluddy arm, man.

I flang my gun wi' a' my might,
   An' fellt his neiper teet, man;
Tan trew my sord, an' at a straik
   Hew't aff te haf o's heet, man.
Pe vain to tell o' a' my tricks;
   My oons pe nae tisgrace, man;
Ekseppin ane akross my hips,
   Ter a' before my face, man.

Frae Roman, Saxon, Pick, an' Dane,
   We hae cot muckle skaith, man;
Yet still te Scot has kept his ain,
   In spite o' their teeth, man.
Ten rouse, my lads, an' fear nae fae;
   For if ye're keen an' true, man,
Although te French pe sax time mae,
   She'll never konker you, man.

I'm auld an' stiff, an', owr my staff,
   Can gang but unco slaw, man;
But sood te Frenchman be sae taft
   As venter here awa, man,

My sord, tat now is auld an' plunt,
  I'll sharp upon a stane, man,
An' hirple toon unto te kost,
  An' faucht for Shorge an' fame, man.

———◆———

MY NATIVE ISLE.

Tune—*Sir Alex. Macdonald Lochart's Strathspey.*

AND must I leave my native Isle ;
Fair friendship's eye, affection's smile ;
The mountain sport, the angler's wile,
  The birch and weeping willow, O !
The Highland glen, the healthy gale,
The gloaming glee, the evening tale ;
And must I leave my native vale,
  And brave the boisterous billow, O !

How sweet to climb the mountain high,
While dawning gilds the eastern sky ;
Or in the shade at noon to lie
  Upon the fell so airy, O.
And, when the sun is sinking low
Through woodland walks to wander slow ;
Or kindly in my plaid to rowe
  My gentle rosy Mary, O.

My native Isle! I love thee well;
I love thee more than I can tell:
Accept my last, my sad farewell;
    In thee I may not tarry, O,
What makes my bosom heave so high?
What makes the dewdrop gild mine eye?
Alas! that dew would quickly dry,
    If 'twere not for my Mary, O!

O youth! thou season light and gay,
How soon thy pleasures melt away!
Like dream dispell'd by dawning day,
    Or waking wild vagary, O.
The thrush shall quit the woodland dale,
The lav'rock cease the dawn to hail,
Ere I forget my native vale,
    Or my sweet lovely Mary, O!

— • —

BUCCLEUCH'S BIRTHDAY.

Tune—*Macfarlane's Reel.*

O FY let's a' be merry, boys,
    O fy let's a' be merry.
This is a day we should rejoice;
    Then fy let's a' be merry.
Our auld gudeman is hale an' free,
    An' that should surely cheer us;

An' the flowers o' a' the south countrie
   Are sweetly smiling near us.
      Our day's nae done though it be dark;
        Put round the Port an' Sherry;
      An' ask at James o' the 'Tower o' Sark,
        If we should nae a' be merry.

Blest be the day the Scot did gain
   His name, and a' surrounding,
" When in the cleuch the buck was ta'en,"
   While hound and horn was sounding.
But ten times blessed be this day
   That brought us noble Harry;
A nation's pride, a country's stay,
  A friend that disna vary.
      Then let's be merry ane an' a',
        An' drink the Port an' Sherry;
      An' spier at George o' the Carterha',
        If we should nae a' be merry.

Then let us drink to brave Buccleuch,
   An' our auld honest Geordie :
For, seek the country through an' through,
   We'll light on few sae worthy :
The one protects our native land,
   And on the sea keeps order ;
The other guides the farmer's hand,
   And rules the Scottish Border.

Then merry, merry, let us be,
   An' drink the Port an' Sherry;
I'll refer to Wat i' the Frostylee,*
   If we should nae a' be merry.

HIGHLAND HARRY BACK AGAIN.†

Ye Forest flowers so fresh and gay,
   Let all your hearts be light and fain;
For once this blest, auspicious day,
   Brought us a Harry back again.
The wild bird's hush'd on Ettrick braes,
   And northward turns the nightly wain;
Let's close with glee this wale of days,
   To us so welcome back again.

May blessings wait that noble Scott,
   Who loves to hear the shepherd's strain;
And long, in peace, may't be his lot
   To see this day come back again.

* The above song was composed and sung at the celebration of the Duke of Buccleuch's birthday at Langholm. The three gentlemen referred to, were Messrs. James Church, George Park, and Walter Bothwick, managers of the ball for that year, 1809.

† This and the two following songs were composed for, and sung at, the celebration of the Earl of Dalkeith's birthday, at Selkirk, on the 24th May.

His heart so kind, his noble mind,
   His loyal course without a stain,
And choice's fair, all, all declare
   He'll just be Harry back again.

———•———

HAP AN' ROWE THE FEETIE O'T.

Tune—*Grant's Rant.*

Gae hap an' rowe the feetie o't;
Gae hap an' rowe the feetie o't;
We'll never trow we hae a bairn
Unless we hear the greetie o't.
Auld fashion'd bodies whine an' tell,
   In prophecies precarious,
That our young Charley never will
   Be sic a man as Harry was.
Auld Harry was an honest man,
   An' nouther flush nor snappy, O;
An' a' the gear that e'er he wan
   Was spent in makin' happy, O.
             Gae hap an' rowe, &c.

There grew a tree at our house-end,
   We hack'd it down, for fire, O;
An', frae the root, there did ascend
   A straughter ane an' higher, O:

Then what's to hinder our young blade,
   When sic a simple's shown him, O,
To trace the steps his father gaed,
   An' e'en to gang beyon' them, O?
                    Gae hap an' rowe, &c.

This day we'll chime in canty rhyme
   What spirit we wad hae him, O;
An' if he run as he's begun,
   Our blessin' aye we'll gie him, O:
We wish him true unto his king,
   An' for his country ready, O;
A steady friend, a master kind,
   An' nouther blate nor greedy, O.
                    Gae hap an' rowe, &c.

While he shall grace the noble name,
   We'll drink his health in Sherry, O;
An' aye this day we'll dance an' play
   In reels an' jigs sae merry, O:
But if it's ken'd his actions tend
   To ony ill-behavin', O,
This bonny twenty-fourth o' May
   In crape we's a' be wavin', O.
     Gae hap an' rowe the feetie o't;
     Gae hap an' rowe the feetie o't;
     We' aye believe 'tis but a bairn
     If ance we hear the greetie o't.

BORN. LADDIE.

TUNE—*Somebody.*

LET wine gae round, an' music play,
This is the twenty-fourth o' May;
An' on this bonny blythsome day
  Our young gudeman was born, laddie,
The Esk shall dance an' Teviot sing,
The Yarrow's bonny banks shall ring,
An' Ettrick's music shall streek her wing,
  This day that he was born, laddie.
    Born, laddie! born, laddie!
    Ilka e'en an' morn, laddie,
    We will bless the happy day
    When Charley he was born, laddie.

May health an' happiness attend
The chief, for truth an' honour ken'd!
An' may he never want a friend,
  To cheer him when forlorn, laddie!
To him an' his we're a' in debt,
An' lang hae been, an' will be yet;
But may he thrive till we forgot
  The day when he was born, laddie;
              Born, laddie, &c.

But should he stern misfortune find,
Then may he calmly call to mind,

'Tis but the lot of all mankind
　　That ever yet were born, laddie.
If pride shall e'er his bosom swell,
An' kindness frae his heart repel,
'Twill mind him, he maun die himsel',
　　As sure as he was born, laddie.
　　　　　　　Born, laddie, &c.

DONALD MACDONALD,

TUNE—*Woo'd an' married an' a'*.

My name it is Donald Macdonald,
　　I live in the Highlands sae grand ;
I've follow'd our banner, an' will do,
　　Wharever my Maker has land.
When rankit amang the blue bonnets,
　　Nae danger can fear me awa ;
I ken that my brethren around me
　　Are neither to conquer or fa'.
　　　　Brogs an' brochen an' a'
　　　　Brochen an' brogs an' a',
　　　　An' isna the laddie weel aff
　　　　Wha has brogs an' brochen an' a ?

Short syne we war wonderfu' canty
　　Our friends an' our country to see ;

But since the proud Consul's grown vauity,
   We'll meet him by land or by sea.
Wherever a clan is disloyal,
   Wherever our king has a foe,
He'll quickly see Donald Macdonald
   Wi' his Highlanders all in a row.
     Guns an' pistols an' a',
     Pistols an' guns an' a';
     He'll quickly see Donald Macdonald
     Wi' guns an' pistols an' a'.

What though we befriendit young Charlie ?
   To tell it I dinna think shame;
Poor lad! he came to us but barely,
   An' reckon'd our mountain his hame :
' Tis true that our reason forbade us,
   But tenderness carried the day ;
Had Geordie come friendless amang us,
   Wi' him we had a' gane away.
     Sword an' buckler an' a',
     Buckler an' sword an' a' :
     For George we'll encounter the devil
     Wi' sword an' buckler an' a'.

An' O I would eagerly press him
   The keys o' the East to retain ;
For should he gie up the possession.
   We'll soon hae to force them again :
Than yield up an inch wi' dishonour,
   Though it war my finishin' blow,

He aye may depend on Macdonald,
  Wi's Highlandmen all in a row.
    Knees an' elbows an' a',
    Elbows an' knees an' a'
    Depend upon Donald Macdonald,
    His knees an' elbows an' a'.

If Bonapart land at Fort-William,
  Auld Europe nae longer shall grane:
I laugh, when I think how we'll gall him
  Wi' bullet, wi' steel, an' wi' stane;
Wi' rocks o' the Nevis an' Gairy
  We'll rattle him aff frae the shore;
Or lull him asleep in a cairney,
  An' sing him " Lochaber no more!"
    Stanes an' bullets an' a';
    Bullets an' stanes an' a'.
    We'll finish the Córsican callan,
    Wi' stanes an' wi' bullets an' a'.

The Gordon is gude in a hurry,
  An' Campbell is steel to the bane;
An' Grant, an' Mackenzie, an' Murray,
  An' Cameron will burkle to nane;
The Stuart is sturdy an' wannle,
  An' sae is Macleod an' Mackay;
An' I their gudebrither Macdonald,
  Sal never be last i' the fray.
    Brogs an' brochen an' a',
    Brochen an' brogs an' a',

An' up wi' the bonny blue bonnet,
The kilt an' the feather an' a'.

BY A BUSH.

TUNE—*Maid that tends the Goats.*

By a bush on yonder brae,
　Where the airy Benger rises,
Sandy tun'd his artless lay ;
Thus he sung the lee-lang day :—
Thou sh'alt ever be my theme,
　Yarrow, winding down the hollow,
With thy bonny sister stream
　　Sweeping through the broom so yellow.
　　　On these banks thy waters lave,
　　　Oft the warrior found a grave.

Oft on thee the silent wain
　Saw the Douglas' banners streaming
Oft on thee the hunter train
Sought the shelter'd deer in vain ;
Oft, in thy green dells and bowers,
　Swains have seen the fairies riding :
Oft the snell and sleety showers
　　Found in thee the warrior hiding.
　　　Many a wild and bloody scene
　　　On thy bonny banks have been.

Now, the days of discord gane,
  Henry's kindness keeps us cheery ;
While his heart shall warm remain,
Dule will beg a hauld in vain.
Bloodless now, in many hues
  Flow'rets bloom, our hills adorning,
There my Jenny milks her ewes,
  Fresh an' ruddy as the morning :
    Mary Scot could could ne'er outvie
    Jenny's hue an' glancing eye.

Wind, my Yarrow, down the howe,
  Forming bows o' dazzling silver ;
Meet thy titty yont the knowe :
Wi' my love I'll join like you.
Flow, my Etrick, it was thee
  Into life wha first did drap me :
Thee I've sung, an' when I dee
  Thou wilt lend a sod to hap me.
    Passing swains shall say, and weep,
    Here our Shepherd lies asleep.

17

THE EMIGRANT.

Air—Lochaber no more.

May morning had shed her red streamers on high,
O'er Canada, frowning all pale on the sky ;
Still dazzling and white was the robe that she wore,
Except where the mountain-wave dash'd on the
      shore.
Far heav'd the young sun, like a lamp, on the wave
And loud scream'd the gull o'er his foam-beaten
      cave,
When an old lyart swain on a headland stood high,
With the staff in his hand, and the tear in his eye.
His old tartan plaid, and his bonnet so blue,
Declar'd from what country his lineage he drew;
His visage so wan, and his accents so low,
Announc'd the companion of sorrow and woe.
" Ah, welcome, thou sun, to thy canopy grand,
And to me ! for thou com'st from my dear native
      land !
Again dost thou leave that sweet isle of the sea,
To beam on these winter-bound vallies and me !

" How sweet in my own native valley to roam !
Each face was a friend's, and each house was a
      home,
To drag our live thousands from river or bay ;
Or chase the dun dear o'er the mountains so gray.

Here daily I wander to sigh on the steep ;
My old bosom friend was laid low in yon deep ;
My family and friends, to extremity driven,
Contending for life both with earth and with heaven.

" My country, they said—but they told me a lie—
Her vallies were barren, inclement her sky ;
Even now in the glens, 'mong her mountains so
     blue,
The primrose and daisy are blooming in dew.
How could she expel from those mountains of
     health
The clans who maintain'd them in danger and
     death !
Who ever were ready the broad-sword to draw
In defence of her honour, her freedom, and law.

" We stood by our Stuart, till one fatal blow
Loos'd Ruin triumphant, and Valour laid low.
Our chief, whom we trusted, and liv'd but to please,
Then turn'd us adrift to the storms and the seas.
O gratitude ! where did'st thou linger the while ?
What region afar is illum'd with thy smile ?
That orb of the sky for a home will I crave,
When yon sun rises red on the Emigrant's grave."

HONEST DUNCAN.

Now wha is yon comes o'er the knowe,
  Sae stalwart an' sae brawny?
His hurchin beard, an' towzy pow,
  Bespeak some Highland Sawny.
We'll hurt his spirit if we can,
  Wi' taunt or jibe uncivil;
Before I saw a Highlandman,
  I'd rather see the devil.

"Now wha are ye wi' tartan trews?
  Or whare hae ye been reaving?
Nae doubt, to cleed your naked houghs
  In England ye've been thieving."
"She no pe heed you, shentlemen,
  Te whisky mak you trunken;
But when I'm in the Athol glen,
  Te ca' me 'onest Duncan."

"An honest man in Athol glen!
  We fear there's ne'er anither.
Nae wonder ye're sae lank an' lean,
  Where a' are knaves thegither."
"Hu, shay, Cot damn, say tat akain.
  Of her you might pe speakin';
But try misca' my countrymen,
  I'll smash you like a breaken."

From words, the blows began to pass;
  Stout Duncan sair laid on 'em;
At length he tumbled on the grass,
  Wi' a' his faes aboon him.
But soon he rais'd his dusty brow,
  An' bellow'd aiths right awfu':
Then whippit out a lang *sken-dhu*,
  An' threaten'd things unlawfu'.

Then he ran here, an' he ran there,
  The Highland durk sae fley'd 'em;
But Duncan chas'd, wi' hurdies bare,
  An' ane by ane repaid 'em.
His Highland durk, an' heavy licks,
  Soon taught them wha they strove wi';
An' he brought part o' a' their breeks
  To Scotland for a trophy.

" Now, you at nakit doups may laugh,
  An' ye'll get some to join ye;
But troth you no maun cang to scaff
  At tough auld Caledony.
Pe mony lad in Athol glen
  Will join you like a brither;
But should you laugh at Highlandmen,
  She a' tak low thegither."

PRINCE OWEN AND THE SEER.

To an old Welsh Air.

"O say, mighty Owen, why beams thy bright
    eye ?
And why shakes thy plume, when the winds
    are so still ?
What means the loud blast of the bugle so nigh ?
    And the wild warlike music I hear on the hill ?"
"We are free, thou old Seer; the Britons are
    free !
Our foes have all fallen, or shrunk from our
    view ;
And free as the bird of the mountain are we,
The roe of the forest, or fish of the sea.
    My country ! my brethren ! my joy is for you,
    My country ! my brethren ! my country ! my
        brethren !
    My country ! my brethren ! my joy is for you."

"Brave Owen ! my old heart is fired by thine !
    My dim eyes they glisten like tears of the morn.
Thy valour us guarded; thy wisdom us warded
    The danger that threaten'd to lay us forlorn.
And when you and I have sunk into our graves !
    When ages o'er ages, Time's standard shall
        rear ;

When the bards have forgot o'er our ashes to
          weep ;
When they scarcely can point out the place where
          we sleep :
  That freedom shall flourish we've purchas'd so
          dear ;
  That freedom shall flourish, &c.

" The Arm that created our shores and our glens,
    Design'd they unconquer'd should ever remain ;
That Power, who inspir'd the hearts of our clans,
    Design'd them, inviolate, their rights to main-
          tain.
Our castle, the mountain ; our bulwark, the wave ;
    The *courage* and *jealousy*, buckler and shield ;
We'll laugh at the force of the world combin'd,
And oppression shall fly like the cloud in the wind.
    But the isles and the ocean to Britain must yield;
    The isles and the ocean ; the isles and the ocean ,
    The isles and the ocean to Britons must yield.'

——————◆——————

HIGHLAND LADDIE.

" WERE ye at Drummossie moor,
    Bonny laddie, Highland laddie ?
Saw ye the Duke the clans o'erpower,
    Bonny laddie, Highland laddie ?"

" Yes, I have seen that fatal fray,
    Bonny laddie, Highland laddie;
And my heart bleeds from day to day,
    Bonny laddie, Highland laddie.

" Many a lord of high degree,
    Bonny laddie, Highland laddie,
Will never more their mountains see,
    Bonny laddie, Highland laddie;
Many a chief of birth and fame,
    Bonny laddie, Highland laddie,
Are hunted down like savage game,
    Bonny laddie, Highland laddie.

" What could the remnant do but yield,
    Bonny laddie, Highland laddie?
A generous chief twice gains the field,
    Bonny laddie, Highland laddie.
Posterity will ne'er us blame,
    Bonny laddie, Highland laddie;
But brand with blood the Brunswick name,
    Bonny laddie, Highland laddie.

" O may it prove for Scotland's good!
    Bonny laddie, Highland laddie.
But why so drench our glens with blood!
    Bonny laddie, Highland laddie.
Duke William nam'd, or yonder moor,
    Bonny laddie, Highland laddie,.

Will fire our blood for evermore,
  Bonny laddie, Highland laddie.''

CALEDONIA.

AIR—*Lord Aboyne.*

CALEDONIA! thou land of the mountain and rock;
  Of the ocean, the mist, and the wind:
Thou land of the torrent, the pine, and the oak;
  Of the roe-buck, the heart, and the hind:
Though bare are thy cliffs, and though barren thy
      glens;
  Though bleak thy dun islands appear;
Yet kind are the hearts, and undaunted the clans,
  That roam on those mountains so drear.

Thou land of the bay, and the headland so steep;
  Of the eagle that hovers on high
O'er the still lake, where, etch'd on his bosom,
      asleep
  Lie the mountain, the cloud, and the sky.
Thou land of the valley, the moor and the hill;
  Of the storm, and the proud rolling wave;
Yes, thou art the land of fair liberty still!
  And the land of my forefathers' grave.

A foe from abroad, or a tyrant at home,
  Could never thy ardour restrain;

The invincible bands of imperial Rome
   Assay'd thy proud spirit in vain.
Firm seat of religion, of valour, of truth,
   Of genius unshackled and free;
The Muses have left all the vales of the south,
   My lov'd Caledonia, for thee.

THE WEE HOUSE.

I LIKE the weel, my wee auld house,
   Tho' laigh thy wa's an' flat the riggin,
Though round thy lum the sourock grows,
   An' rain-draps gaw by cozy biggin',
Lang hast thou happit mine and me,
   My head's grown gray aneath thy kipple,
And aye the ingle cheek was free
   Baith to the blind man an' the cripple.

What gart my ewes thrive on the hill,
   An' kept my little store increasin'?
The rich man never wish'd me ill,
   The poor man left me aye his blessin'.
Troth I maun greet wi' thee to part,
   Though to a better house I'm flittin';
Sic joys will never glad my heart
   As I've had by this hallan sittin'.

My bonny bairns around me smiled
　My sonsy wife sat by me spinning,
Aye lilting o'er her ditties wild,
　In notes sae artless an' sae winning.
Our frugal meal was aye a feast,
　Our e'ening psalm a hymn of joy;
Sae calm an' peacefu' was our rest,
　Our bliss, our love, without alloy.

I canna help but haud the dear,
　My auld storm-batter'd, homely shieling;
Thy sooty lum, an' kipples clear
　I better love than gaudy ceiling.
Thy roof will fa', thy rafters start,
　How damp an' cauld thy earth will be!
Ah! sae will soon ilk honest heart,
　That erst was blythe and bauld in thee!

I thought to cower aneath thy wa',
　'Till death should close my weary een,
Then leave thee for the narrow ha',
　Wi' lowly roof o' sward sae green.
Fareweel my house an' burnie clear,
　My bourtree bush an' bowzy tree!
The wee while I maun sojourn here,
　I'll never find a hame like thee.

EXTRACTS

FROM

THE QUEEN'S WAKE, &c.

269

EXTRACTS.

THE RETURN OF THE BURIED ONE.

'Twas late, late on a Sabbath night!
At the hour of the ghost, and the restless sprite!
The mass at Carelha' had been read,
And all the mourners were bound to bed,
When a foot was heard on the paved floor,
And a gentle rap came to the door.

O God! that such a ray should be
So fraught with ambiguity!
A dim haze clouded every sight;
Each hair had life and stood upright;
No sound was heard throughout the hall,
But the beat of the heart and the cricket's call;
So deep the silence imposed by fear,
That a vacant buzz sang in the ear.

The lady of Carelha' first broke
The breathless hush, and thus she spoke:
" Christ be our shield! who walks so late,
And knocks so gently at my gate?

271

I felt a pang—it was not dread—
It was the memory of the dead.
O! death is a dull and dreamless sleep!
The mould is heavy, the grave is deep!
Else I had ween'd that foot so free
The step and the foot of my Mary Lee!
And I had ween'd that gentle knell
From the light hand of my daughter fell!
The grave is deep, it may not be!
Haste porter—haste to the door and see."

He took the key with an eye of doubt,
He lifted the lamp, and he look'd about ;
His lips a silent prayer address'd,
And the cross was sign'd upon his breast ;
Thus mail'd within, the armour of God,
All ghostly to the door he strode.
He wrench'd the bolt with grating din,
He lifted the latch—but none came in !
He thrust out his lamp, and he thrust out his head,
And he saw the face and the robes of the dead !
One sob he heaved, and tried to fly,
But he sank on the earth, and the form came by.

She enter'd the hall, she stood in the door,
Till one by one dropp'd on the floor,
The blooming maiden, and matron old,
The friar gray, and the yeoman bold.
It was like a scene on the Border green,
When the arrows fly and pierce unseen ;

And nought was heard within the hall,
But Aves, vows, and groans, withal.
The lady of Carel' stood alone,
But moveless as a statue of stone.

"O! lady mother, thy fears forego;
Why all this terror and this woe?
But late when I was in this place,
Thou would'st not look me in the face;
O! why do you blench at sight of me?
I am thy own child, thy Mary Lee."

"I saw thee dead and cold as clay;
I watch'd thy corpse for many a day;
I saw thee laid in the grave at rest;
I strew'd the flowers upon thy breast;
And I saw the mould heap'd over thee—
Thou art not my child, my Mary Lee."

O'er Mary's face amazement spread;
She knew not that she had been dead;
She gazed in mood irresolute:
Both stood aghast, and both were mute.
From the Pilgrims of the Sun.

18

INVOCATION.

Thou holy harp of Judah's land,
 That hung the willow boughs upon,
O leave the bowers on Jordan's strand
 And cedar groves of Lebanon:

That I may sound thy sacred string,
 Those chords of mystery sublime,
That chimed the songs of Israel's King,
 Song that shall triumph over time.

Pour forth the tracing notes again,
 That wont of yore the soul to thrill,
In tabernacles of the plain,
 Or heights of Zion's holy hill.

O come, ethereal timbrel meet,
 In shepherd's hand thou dost delight;
On Kedar hills thy strain was sweet,
 And sweet on Bethle'm's plain by night.

And when thy tones the land shall hear,
 And every heart conjoins with thee,
The mountain lyre that lingers near
 Will lend a wandering melody.
      From the Pilgrims of the Sun.

QUEEN MARY'S RETURN TO SCOT-LAND.

AFTER a youth my woes o'ercast,
After a thousand sorrows past,
The lovely Mary once again
Set foot upon her native plain;
Knelt on the pier with modest grace,
And turn'd to Heaven her beauteous face.
'Twas then the caps in air were blended,
A thousand thousand shouts ascended,
Shiver'd the breeze around the throng,
Gray barrier cliffs the peals prolong,
And every tongue gave thanks to Heaven,
That Mary to their hopes was given.

Her comely form and graceful mien
Bespoke the lady and the queen;
The woes of one so fair and young,
Moved every heart and every tongue.
Driven from her home a helpless child,
To brave the winds and billows wild;
An exile bred in realms afar,
Amid commotions, broils, and war.
In one short year, her hopes all cross'd—
A parent, husband, kingdom, lost!
And all ere eighteen years had shed
Their honours o'er her royal head.

For such a queen, the Stuarts' heir—
A queen so courteous, young, and fair—
Who would not every foe defy?
Who would not stand—who would not die?

Light on her airy steed she sprung,
Around with golden tassels hung;
No chieftain there rode half so free,
Or half so light and gracefully.
How sweet to see her ringlets pale
Wide waving in the southland gale,
Which through the broom-wood blossoms flew,
To fan her cheeks of rosy hue!
Where'er it heaved her bosom's screen,
What beauties in her form were seen!
And when her courser's mane it swung,
A thousand silver bells were rung.
A sight so fair, on Scottish plain,
A Scot shall never see again!

When Mary turn'd her wond'ring eyes
On rocks that seem'd to prop the skies;
On palace, park, and battled pile;
On lake, on river, sea, and isle;
O'er woods and meadows bathed in dew,
To distant mountains wild and blue;
She thought the isle that gave her birth,
The sweetest, wildest land on earth.

From The Queen's Wake.

THE LADY AND THE FIELD OF BAT-
TLE.

WHAT vision lingers on the heath,
Flitting across the field of death ?
Its gliding motion, smooth and still
As vapour on the twilight hill,
Or the last ray of falling even
Shed through the parting clouds of heaven ?

Is it a sprite that roams forlorn ?
Or angel from the bowers of morn,
Come down a tear of heaven to shed,
In pity o'er the valiant dead ?
No vain, no fleeting phantom this !
No vision from the bowers of bliss !
Its radiant eye and stately tread
Bespeak some beauteous mountain maid ;
No rosé of Eden's bosom meek,
Could match that maiden's moisten'd cheek ;
No drifted wreath of morning snow
The whiteness of her lofty brow ;
Nor gem of India's purest dye,
The lustre of her eagle eye.

When beauty, Eden's bowers within,
First stretch'd the arm to deeds of sin ;
When passion burn'd, and prudence slept,
The pitying angels bent and wept.

But tears more soft were never shed,
No, not when angels bow'd the head,
A sigh more mild did never breathe
O'er human nature whelm'd in death,
Nor woe and dignity combine
In face so lovely, so benign,
As Douglas saw that dismal hour,
Bent o'er a corse on Cample-moor—
A lady o'er her shield, her trust,
A brave, an only brother's dust.

What heart of man unmoved can lie,
When plays the smile in beauty's eye?
Or when a form of grace and love
To music's notes can lightly move?
Yes; there are hearts unmoved can see
The smile, the ring, the revelry;
But heart of warrior ne'er could bear
The beam of beauty's crystal tear.
Well was that morn the maxim proved—
The Douglas saw, the Douglas loved.

From The Queen's Wake.

THE HARP OF SCOTLAND.

Long has that harp, of magic tone,
To all the minstrel world been known:

Who has not heard her witching lays,
Of Ettrick banks and Yarrow braes?
But that sweet bard, who sung and pray'd
Of many a feat and border raid,
Of many a knight and lovely maid,
When forced to leave his harp behind,
Did all her tuneful chords unwind;
And many ages pass'd and came
Ere man so well could tune the same.

Bangour the daring task essay'd:
Not half the chords his fingers play'd;
Yet even then some thrilling lays
Bespoke the harp of ancient days.

Redoubted Ramsay's peasant skill
Flung some strain'd notes along the hill;
His was some lyre from lady's hall,
And not the mountain harp at all.

Langhorne arrived from southern dale,
And chimed his notes on Yarrow vale;
They would not, could not, touch the heart—
His was the modish lyre of art.

Sweet rung the harp to Logan's hand:
Then Leyden came from border land,
With dauntless heart and ardour high,
And wild impatience in his eye.

Though false his tones at times might be,
Though wild notes marr'd the symphony
Between, the glowing measure stole
That spoke the bard's inspired soul.
Sad were those strains, when hymn'd afar,
On the green vales of Malabar:
O'er seas beneath the golden morn
They travell'd, on the monsoon borne,
Thrilling the heart of Indian maid,
Beneath the wild banana's shade.
Leyden, a shepherd wails thy fate,
And Scotland knows her loss too late.

The day arrived—blest be the day,
Walter the Abbot came that way!
The sacred relic met his view—
Ah! well the pledge of heaven he knew.
He screw'd the chords, he tried a strain;
'Twas wild—he tuned and tried again;
Then pour'd the numbers bold and free,
The simple magic melody.

The land was charm'd to list his lays;
It knew the harp of ancient days.
The border chiefs, that long had been
In sepulchres unhearsed and green,
Pass'd from their mouldy vaults away,
In armour red, and stern array,

And by their moonlight halls were seen,
In visor, helm, and habergeon.
Even fairies sought our land again,
So powerful was the magic strain.

    Blest be his generous heart for aye !
He told me where the relic lay ;
Pointed my way with ready will,
Afar on Ettrick's wildest hill ;
Watch'd my first notes with curious eye,
And wonder'd at my minstrelsy :
He little ween'd a parent's tongue
Such strains had o'er my cradle sung.

                       From The Queen's Wake.

STAFFA.

But now the dreadful strand they gain,
Where rose the sacred dome of the main ;
Oft had they seen the place before,
And kept aloof from the dismal shore,
But now it rose before their prow,
And what they beheld they did not know.
The tall gray forms, in close-set file,
Upholding the roof of that holy pile ;
The sheets of foam and the clouds of spray,
And the groans that rush'd from the portals gray,
Appall'd their hearts and drove them away.

They wheel'd their bark to the east around,
And moor'd in basin, by rocks imbound;
They awed to silence, they trode the strand
Where furnaced pillars in order stand,
All framed in the liquid burning levin,
And bent like the bow that spans the heaven,
Or upright ranged in horrid array,
With purfle of green o'er the darksome gray.

Their path was on wondrous pavement of old,
Its blocks all cast in some giant mould,
Fair hewn and grooved by no mortal hand,
With countermure guarded by sea and by land.
The watcher Bushella frown'd over their way,
Enrobed in the sea-baize, and hooded with gray;
The warder that stands by that dome of the deep.
With spray-shower and rainbow, the entrance to
        keep.
But when they drew nigh to the chancel of ocean,
And saw her waves rush to their raving devotion,
Astounded and awed to the antes they clung,
And listen'd the hymns in her temple she sung.
The song of the cliff, when the winter winds blow,
The thunder of heaven, the earthquake below,
Conjoin'd, like the voice of a maiden would be,
Compared with the anthem there sung by the sea.

The solemn rows in that darksome den,
Where dimly seen like the forms of men,

Like giant monks in ages agone,
Whom the God of the ocean had sear'd to stone,
And bound in his temple for ever to lean,
In sackcloth of gray and visors of green,
An everlasting worship to keep,
And the big salt tears eternally weep.

So rapid the motion, the whirl, and the boil,
So loud was the tumult, so fierce the turmoil,
Appalled from those portals of terror they turn,
On pillar of marble their incense to burn.
Around the holy flame they pray—
Then turning their faces all west away,
On angel pavement each bent his knee,
And sung this hymn to the God of the sea.

From The Queen's Wake.

———————◆———————

KILMENY'S RECEPTION BY THE FAIRIES.

They claspit her weste and handis fayre,
They kissit her cheik, and they kembit her hayir;
And runde cam ilka blumyng fere,
Sayn, "Bonnye Kilmeny, ye're welcome here!
Wemyn are freeit of the littand scorne—
Oh, blest be the daye Kilmeny was born!

Now shall the land of the spiritis see,
Now shall it ken quhat ane womyn may be!
Mony long eir, in sorrow and pain,
Mony lang eir thro' the worild we haif gane,
Comyshonit to watch fayir womynkinde,
For it's they quha nurice the immortyl minde,
We haif watchit their stepis as the dawnyng shone,
And deip in the greinwudde walkis alone,
By lilye bouir, and silken bedde,
The viewless teiris haif ouir them shedde;
Haif soothit their ardent myndis to sleep,
Or left the cuche of luife to weip.
We haif sein! we have sein!—but the tyme mene
          come,
And the angelis will blush at the day of doom!

Oh, wald the fayrest of mortyl kynde
Aye keipe thilke holye troths in mynde—
That kyndred spiritis ilk motion see,
Quha watch their wayis with anxious e'e,
And grieve for the guilt of humanitye!
Oh, sweit to hevin the maydenis prayer,
And the siche that hevis ane bosom se fayre!
And deir to hevin the wordis of truthe,
And the praise of vertu fra beautyis muthe!
And deire to the viewless formis of ayre,
The mynde that kythis as the body fayre

From The Queen's Wake.

A STERN FATHER'S LATE REPENT-
ANCE.

THAT morning found rough Tushilaw
　In all the father's guise appear;
An end of all his hopes he saw
　Shrouded in Mary's gilded bier.

No eye could trace without concern
　The suffering warrior's troubled look—
The throbs that heav'd his bosom stern
　No ear could bear, no heart could brook.

"¡Woe be to thee, thou wicked dame!
　My Mary's prayers and accents mild
Might well have render'd vengeance lame—
　This hand could ne'er have slain my child.

" But thou, in frenzied fatal hour,
　Reft the sweet life thou gav'st away,
And crush'd to earth the fairest flower
　That ever breathed the breeze of day.

" My all is lost, my hope is fled,
　The sword shall ne'er be drawn for me;
Unblest, unhonour'd, my gray head—
　My child—would I had died for thee!"

The bells toll o'er a new-made grave;
   The lengthen'd funeral train is seen
Stemming the Yarrow's silver wave,
   And dark'ning Dryhope holms so green.
               From The Queen's Wake.

THE HARP OF TEVIOT.

LINES ON THE DEATH OF DR. JOHN LEYDEN.

WHY weeps the poplar o'er the stream?
   Why wails the chilly winter gale?
Why starts the peasant from his dream
   Adown the links of Teviotdale?

What strain was that so wild, so sweet,
   A hymn of heaven that strain must be,
To theme so thrilling, wo so sweet,
   So soft the midnight melody!

It flows not from yon streamer pale,
   Nor from the window'd choirs of bliss;
Ye maidens fair of Teviotdale,
   What wild, what wondrous song is this?

A thoughtful shepherd, fair and young,
   Upraised his head to list the strain;
And aye it rung, and aye it sung;
   But every note was fraught with pain.

Full well the fairy sound he knew;
  It waver'd from the poplar pale,
Where parting genius weeping threw
  The magic Harp of Teviotdale.

So sweetly down the dale it rung,
  The breeze of midnight died away,
The falcon o'er the poplar hung,
  The fieldfare, and the merlin gray.

The wakeful cock forgot to crow,
  The snow-birds flocked around the tree,
And ravish'd, sunk in trance of woe,
  Thrilled by the melting melody.

It rang so low, it rang so long,
  Few were the notes the youth could hear,
But aye the burden of the song
  Was, " Soundly sleeps my Minstrel dear."

" The gray moss o'er my strings shall spread;
  My notes must die adown the vale,
Since lowly lies the Minstrel's head
  That tuned the Harp of Teviotdale.

" LEYDEN is fallen, and genius weeps!
  Leyden to me, to nature true;
Sound, sound the bard of Teviot sleeps!
  —Sweet Minstrel of the vale, adieu.

" His lonely grave may balm entwine
  With bandalets so beauteously ;
Weep o'er his dust, the purple vine,
  And wave the wild banana tree.

" Ye spirits of that vernal clime,
  Around his grave your vigils keep,
And wake the choral hymn sublime,
  To soothe my Leyden's slumbers deep ;

" For, ah ! that soul of fire is fled,
  To dream o'er fields of wondrous lore ;
And consecrate my rural reed,
  A Harp of Heaven for evermore.

" Long may the Harp of Teviotdale
  Forgotten on the poplar hang,
Save when the spirits of the vale
  At midnight twang my runic string."

Slow died its wailing sound away ;
  The shepherd sought the poplar pale,
And reached his skilless hand to play
  The heavenly Harp of Teviotdale.

A spirit clove the welkin gray,
  Swift as the motion of the mind ;
The sacred symbol snatch'd away,
  And mounted on the murmuring wind.

Lightning Source UK Ltd.
Milton Keynes UK
UKOW020011131012

200492UK00003B/54/P